Servant of the SHOGUN

RICHARD TAMES, a graduate of Cambridge and London Universities, works at the University of London's School of Oriental and African Studies. He is the author of various works on Japan.

Servant of the SHOGUN

Being the True Story of William Adams,
Pilot and Samurai,
The First Englishman in Japan.

Richard Tames

Paul Norbury Publications Limited
Tenterden, Kent

SERVANT OF THE SHOGUN

PAUL NORBURY PUBLICATIONS LTD

Caxton House, High Street, Tenterden, Kent, England

First published 1981

© Richard Tames

All rights reserved. No part of this publication may be reproduced, stored in a retrieval system, or transmitted in any form or by any means without prior permission of the copyright owner. Enquiries should be directed to the publishers.

ISBN 0 904404 39 0

Set in Times Roman 11 on 12 pt.
Printed in Great Britain by A. Wheaton & Co. Ltd, Exeter

To
Hiroshi Otah
Jutaro Sakamoto
Tomoko Katsuno

About Quotations

This book relies heavily on surviving historical documents — letters, journals and diaries written in English, Dutch, Portuguese, Spanish and Japanese. So acute are the observations contained in these documents, and so much do they reveal about the various writers, who were more often than not participants in the events related here, that I have woven scores of separate quotations into my text. I have chosen not to give a source indication for each extract, but I do list the major references in a bibliographical note at the back. I have also taken the liberty of modernizing the spellings and standardizing the appearance of words in the quoted texts. I have, however, changed neither the words per se nor the style of punctuation. And I have allowed most place names and personal names to stand as in the original, even though this sometimes results in their appearing in more than one form.

R.T.

Contents

Preface
'I am a Kentish man'
'We sett sayle'
'This Island of Iapon'
'The principal king'
'Tighten the strings'
'Grace and favour'
'The governor of Manilia'
'Discreet friend, Willem Adams'
'Let them inquir for me'
'A naturalized Japanner'
'The King of Englans letter'
'To go for my country'
'In the General's absence'
'A profitable servant'
'A voyage to Siam'
'The fortres of Osekey'
'In thear relligion very zellous'
'Com againe to morow'
'But a loosing voyage'
'Much adoe'
'From tooth outward'
'I William Adams mariner'
'Out of hope'
Epilogue
A Note on Sources and Further Reading
Chronology

Preface

'... it seems nature purposely designed these islands to be a sort of a little world, separate and independent of the rest, by making them of so difficult an access, and by endowing them plentifully, with whatever is requisite to make the lives of their inhabitants both delightful and pleasant, and to enable them to subsist without a commerce with foreign nations.'

Thus wrote the German physician Engelbert Kaempfer after a two-year sojourn in Japan in the service of the Dutch East India Company. Kaempfer was writing in the last decade of the seventeenth century. The previous two and a half centuries had seen that immense expansion of European commerce and influence which was to sketch the outlines of today's patterns of global interdependence. Western historians have arrogantly referred to this process and period as the 'Age of Discovery'. It would perhaps be more accurate to rename it the 'Age of Encounter', for it involved not merely the exploitation of new maritime skills and the application of cartographic knowledge but also a considerable attempt to master the arts of cultural negotiation, to comprehend and manipulate not only the languages of strange peoples but also their manners, customs and prejudices.

By no means did every society yield readily to the penetration of European commerce, products, fashions and beliefs. And no society reacted more vigorously, both in accepting and rejecting alien culture, than did Japan. In less than a century, between 1543, when Europeans blown off course landed just south of the island of Kyushu at Tanegashima, and 1640, when a Portuguese envoy was massacred for attempting to persuade the Japanese to reopen contacts with the outside world, Japan moved from innocent fascination with the 'southern barbarians' to an implacable determination to exclude not merely their physical presence but also their pernicious philosophies.

Standing at the juncture of this remarkable transformation of attitudes we find William Adams, sailor of fortune, a man destined to play a unique and pivotal role in Japanese history. One writer has described him as a small figure who cast a long shadow. But he was in every way a big man, possessed of great energy, as well as great ambition. And it is perhaps a little strange that his shadow should be more clearly seen in his adopted country than in the land of his birth. This book has been written to redress the balance. The story that it tells is not only very remarkable but also entirely true.

1
'I am a Kentish man'

'Your worships, to whom this present writing shall come, is to give you to understand that I am a Kentish man.'
LETTER OF WILLIAM ADAMS, 22 OCTOBER 1611

William Adams was born in 1564, the same year as William Shakespeare. The parish register shows that he was baptized on 24 September. His birthplace in Gillingham, Kent, south-east of London, he describes as 'two English miles from Rochester, one mile from Chattam, where the King's ships do lie'. The absence of surviving papers relating to his family suggests that they were poor people, with neither property nor education. Adam's own education was to be a practical one: 'from the age of twelve years old, I was brought up in Limehouse, near London, being apprentice twelve years to Master Nicholas Diggines'. He completed his apprenticeship in 1588, the year in which Catholic Spain sent a massive invasion fleet against England. Adams played his part in fighting the Armada as captain of the *Richard Duffield*, a supply ship of 120 tons with a crew of twenty-five which brought food and ammunition to the main English battle fleet. The following year, on 20 August, the young pilot married Mary Hyn in the parish church of St. Dunstan's, Stepney, just east of London.

Most of Adam's next ten years were spent at sea, usually in the service of 'the worshipful company of the Barbary merchants', trading with the Muslim kingdoms of North Africa. Turkish seapower in the western Mediterranean had been broken at the great battle of Lepanto in 1571 when the Ottoman navy lost more than 200 galleys; but the seas were still infested with pirates and sailing in them was no matter of mere routine. Even regular trading carried terrible risks. Richard Hakluyt, the diligent chronicler of Elizabethan navigations, records a voyage to 'Tripolis' in 1583 during which a quarrel over customs duties led to the confiscation of the ship and its cargo, the execution of its captain and the enslavement of its entire crew. Despite such dangers the English began in this period to challenge very successfully the Spanish, French and Italians for the rich trade of the region. According to Fernand Braudel, the celebrated historian of the Mediterranean, the English succeeded through perseverance, honest dealing, fine seamanship and superior organization, depending especially upon a highly effective convoy system. But Braudel also notes that the English were not above the occasional act of piracy themselves.

From 1593 to 1595 Adams took part in Dutch expeditions to find a 'north-east passage', by sailing round Arctic Russia, to the 'Spice Islands' of the East Indies. An expedition fitted out by the Merchant Adventurers in 1553 had ended in disaster: 'Sir Hugh Willoughby and all his company died, being frozen to death'. But the potential rewards were so great that repeated efforts were to be made throughout the century. A memorandum drawn up by the merchants of the recently founded Muscovy Company in 1580 outlines some of the incidental benefits to be anticipated from the establishment of an English trading presence on the inhospitable shores of the Arctic seas:

'If you find the soil planted with people, it is like that in time an ample vent [sale] of our warm woollen cloths may be found. And if there be no people at all there to be found, then you shall specially note what plenty of whales, and of other fish is to be found there.... And it may be that the inland may yield masts, pitch, tar, hemp, and all things for the Navy.'

Adams's presence aboard a Dutch ship need occasion no surprise. Trading links between the two rising maritime powers of north-western Europe were strong. Dutch participation in the defeat of the Spanish Armada and English aid for the twenty-year rebellion of the Dutch against Spanish rule created further bonds of friendship and mutual regard. English pilots, moreover, thanks to the strict training imposed by the regulatory body Trinity House since the reign of Henry VIII, were held in the highest esteem. A man of Adams's background and experience would undoubtedly be an asset to any expedition venturing into hazardous and unknown waters.

In fact, two Dutch expeditions were sent out in 1594. An Amsterdam ship, commanded by William Barents, sailed to the north of Novaya Zemlya in Arctic Russia, navigating its west coast as far as 77° north. The merchants of Zeeland, following

The Adams' memorial in Gillingham, Kent, photographed at the time of the unveiling ceremony in 1934 and featuring the old imperial Japanese flag.

Hakluyt's advice, favoured the channel to the south of Novaya Zemlya, pioneered by English explorers. Their ship passed through the Yugor Strait into the Kara Sea. In 1595 a combined expedition, with Barents as chief pilot, failed to penetrate the ice of the Yugor Strait and turned back. Barents led another two-ship expedition the following year and, sailing a more westerly course, discovered Spitsbergen. After the two ships separated, Barents rounded the north-eastern cape of Novaya Zemlya only to have his ship immobilized for the winter in a frozen sea. Having built a hut for shelter, the crew became the first party of Europeans to survive an Arctic winter. When summer came they made their way back in open boats. After surviving such an ordeal it was perhaps ironic that Barents should die of scurvy before reaching home.

The Dutch expeditions failed in their chief objective, to find a north-east passage. There was no way to bypass the Spanish and Portuguese who controlled the routes to the fabulous wealth of Asia. But they had, at much pain, at least disproved the cartographer Mercator's casual claim that 'the voyage to Cathay by the east is doubtless very easy and short'. The experience also enabled Adams to perfect his command of Dutch and it is, therefore, not surprising that when he learned of a Dutch venture to enter the 'Indish traffic' he should be eager to join it and 'make a little experience of the small knowledge which God had given me'.

2

'We sett sayle'

'We set sail with five ships from the Texel, in Holland, the four and twentieth of June 1598.'
LETTER FROM WILLIAM ADAMS TO HIS WIFE; 1611

When Adams and his shipmates sailed from Holland their fleet consisted of five ships — the *Geloof* ('Belief'), the *Blijde Boodschap* ('Good Tidings'), the *Trouw* ('Faith'), the *Liefde* ('Charity') and the *Hoop* ('Hope'). Adams was pilot of the *Hoop* until his transfer to the 160-ton *Liefde*, which as it turned out was the only ship to reach Japan. The *Hoop* was to be lost without trace in the vast reaches of the Pacific just over a year later.

Delay and indecision were to mar the voyage from the outset. Having lost sight of England on 5 July, 1598, the fleet ploughed on toward the equator but, as Adams was to record rancorously a decade later, 'it was too late ere we came to the line, to pass it without contrary winds'. Late in August the expedition made a landfall in the Cape Verde Islands, taking ashore many sick men. Falsely believing that fresh meat, in the form of wild goats, was to be had for the taking, the commanders of the fleet delayed for more than three weeks. At a council of war the pilots of all five ships unanimously pronounced their dislike of the anchorage — 'which were by all the captains taken so ill, that afterward it was agreed by them all, that the pilots should be no more in the council, the which was executed'.

On 15 September the fleet set sail once more. Its overall commander, Jacques Mahu, died shortly thereafter from a prolonged illness. But by then, being buffeted by 'many contrary winds and rain' his erstwhile subordinates were too preoccupied with the question of physical survival to worry over-much about the problems of leadership and decision-making.

Landfall in West Africa at first brought little relief — 'for we could find no store of victuals' — but the Portuguese-controlled island of Annobon (Illha da Nobon) in the Gulf of Guinea offered better prospects. Portuguese attempts to turn away the newcomers were soon defeated by the dispatch of an armed landing party, whose arrival caused the Portuguese to flee inland after firing their own settlement. A second skirmish ended further resistance and the Dutch settled down to land their sick. But, despite the availability of 'oxen, oranges and divers fruits', 'the unwholesomeness of the air was very bad, that as one bettered, another fell sick'. After setting fire to the church and those buildings which still remained standing, the Dutch therefore quit the coast of Africa for the Straits of Magellan.

The voyage across the South Atlantic was accompanied by further severe privations. Men were limited to four ounces of bread per day. Not only wine but even water was rationed — 'which scarcity of victuals brought such feebleness, that our men fell into so great weakness and sickness for hunger, that they did eat the calves' skins wherewith our ropes were covered'. One man died raving, another from the clumsy amputation of his frozen feet. One of the ships had its main-mast swept overboard and 'in the sea with much trouble we set a new mast'.

The Straits of Magellan were finally reached in April 1599. Here the sailors 'laded our boat full of penguins, which are fowls greater than a duck, wherewith we were greatly refreshed'. The advantage of this good fortune was, however, quickly squandered because the new commander of the fleet, ignoring the opportunity of a favourable wind, chose to linger several days searching for wood and water and assembling a prefabricated twenty-ton pinnace. For many the delay was to prove fatal. Opposing winds drove the fleet to seek a safe harbour and to endure months of 'wonderful much snow and ice with great winds' so that 'with cold on the one side and hunger on the other our men grew weaker'. Many died of exposure. Others were murdered by natives when they went ashore to forage for firewood.

Eventually the fleet passed safely through the straits, only to be dispersed by an even greater storm than it had met with so far. The *Geloof*, failing to find her sister ships, met up instead with Oliver van Noort, whose vessel was to be the first Dutch ship to complete the circumnavigation of the world. Provisioned by van Noort, the *Geloof* passed back through the Straits of Magellan, arriving at last in Holland in July 1600, with only thirty-six of her crew alive and most of those perilously close to death. The *Trouw* made for the East Indies, where she was captured by the Portuguese. Six of her crew at last managed to escape from captivity in India and eventually got back to Holland. The *Blijde Boodschap* sailed for the

From a drawing by W. McLaren featuring Adams' ship Liefde and the rest of the Dutch fleet, attacking the Portuguese island of Annobon in the Gulf of Guinea. (Courtesy Harvill Press.)

pre-arranged rendezvous off the coast of Chile and was taken by the Spanish at Valparaiso. The *Liefde* alone kept her assignation, but in vain. After four fruitless weeks she touched the mainland and briefly traded sheep from the natives in return for knives, before they fled inland for fear of the Spanish. After calling at the islands of Mocha and Santa Maria, the *Liefde* turned again towards the mainland of Chile.

Having anchored 'in a fair sandy bay in fifteen fathoms', it was decided to send a party ashore 'to parle [i.e. speak] with the people of the land', the ship's company once more being desperate for food. Braving a shower of arrows, the landing party made clear 'with signs and tokens of friendship' their wish to trade peacefully. Having received small quantities of food and drink, the Dutch thought themselves well understood and retired from their hazardous enterprise with some satisfaction, eager only to conclude their transactions the following day. Adams's own taut description of the ensuing tragedy could scarcely be improved upon:

'The next day, being the 9th of November 1599, our captain, with all our officers, prepared to go a land, having taken counsel to go to the water side, but not to land more than two or three at the most; for there were people in abundance unknown to us: wild, therefore not to be trusted; which counsel being concluded upon, the captain himself did go in one of our boats, with all the force that we could make; and being by the shore side, the people of the country made signs that they should come a land; but that did not well like our captain. In the end, the people not coming near unto our boats, our captain, with the rest, resolved to land, contrary to that which was concluded aboard our ship, before their going a land. At length, three and twenty men landed with muskets, and marched up towards four or five houses, and when they were about a musket shot from the boats, more than a thousand Indians, which lay in ambush, immediately fell upon our men with such weapons as they had, and slew them all to our knowledge. So our boats did long wait to see if any of them did come again; but being all slain, our boats returned: which sorrowful news of all our men's deaths was very much lamented of us all; for we had scarce so many men left as could wind up our anchor.'

Among the dead was Adams's younger brother, Thomas.

The survivors managed to make it back to the island of Santa Maria where, to their great joy, they found the *Hoop* at anchor. The sister ship had also borne its full share of misfortune, 'having lost their general, with seven and twenty of their men, slain at the island of Mocha, from whence they departed the day before we came by'. There were now too few fit men to make up a landing party to go back to the mainland and seize provisions by force. But no other course of action seemed possible. Then, by an incredible stroke of fortune, two Spanish spies were caught and agreed to buy their liberty in return for supplies. This lucky turn of events put the expedition in fresh heart, but reunion had kindled no spirit of unity. A council of war was held at which Adams and the pilot of the *Hoop*, Timothy Shotten, another Englishman, suggested that all the cargo should be put in one ship and the crews amalgamated, the other ship being put to the torch — 'but that the captains were made new, the one nor the other, would not, so that we could not agree to leave the one or the other'. Believing the Spanish to be actively searching for them, the captains therefore decided to leave the hostile coast of 'Perow' and strike out across the Pacific to 'Iapon', 'having understood that cloth was good merchandise there' and accepting the advice of one Dirk Geritszoon (the first Dutchman ever to have visited Japan — in 1585) that 'the most part of the East Indies were hot countries, where woollen cloth would not be much accepted'.

Somewhere in the Pacific eight sailors from the *Liefde* seized its pinnace and fled to an island which, unfortunately for them, was inhabited by cannibals — 'and (as we suppose) were eaten of the wild men'.

On 23 February the two ships encountered 'a wondrous storm of wind . . . with much rain'. On the 24th the *Liefde* lost sight of the *Hoop*, 'which afterward we saw no more'.

Holding fast to her course for Japan, the *Liefde* must have seemed to have been sailing to her doom. 'Great was the misery we were in, having no more but nine or ten able men to go or even creep upon their knees: our captain, and all the rest, looking every hour to die'. Adams failed to achieve his intended landfall 'by reason', as he recorded acidly a decade later, 'that it lieth false in all cards [i.e. charts] and maps and globes'.

But at last, in April 1600, the *Liefde* came in sight of the coast of Japan. By then only 24 of the original crew of 110 were left alive and of these only 6 were strong enough to stand and feebly work the ship. As the *Liefde* lay at anchor off the eastern shores of Kyushu dozens of small boats came bobbing over the sea toward her, 'the people whereof we willingly let come, having no force to resist them. . . .'

3

'This Island of Iapon'

'This Island of Iapon is a great land and lieth to the northwards.'
LETTER OF WILLIAM ADAMS, OCTOBER 1611

The extent of Adams's knowledge of Japan at the time of his landing can only be a matter for speculation, but we do know that English accounts of the country and its people had begun to appear during the reign of Queen Elizabeth toward the end of the sixteenth century. A description of Japan in *The First Booke of Relations of Moderne States* begins with an acute observation of its singularity: 'Japonia may be said to be, as it were, a body of many and sundry islands, of all sorts of bigness; which isles, as they are separated in situation from the rest of the whole world, so are they, in like manner, inhabited of people, most different from all others, both for manners and customs.'

Among these manners and customs the author of this account emphasizes the following: 'a notable wit and incredible patience in suffering, labour and sorrow. They take great and diligent care lest, in word or deed, they should show either fear, or dullness of mind.... They covet exceedingly honour and praise, and poverty with them bringeth no damage to the nobility of blood. They suffer not the least injury in the world to pass unrevenged. For gravity and courtesy they give not place to the Spaniards. They are generally affable and full of compliments. They are very punctual in the entertaining of strangers, of whom they will curiously inquire even trifles of foreign people, as of their manners and such like things. They will as soon lose a limb as omit one ceremony in welcoming a friend.... The most part of them that dwell in cities can write and read. They only study martial feats and are delighted in arms.... The people be fair and very comely of shape. The merchants, although very rich and wealthy, yet nothing account of here; those that are of nobility are greatly esteemed although they be never so poor.'

These observations seem to follow no particular order, but many were to be remarked upon again and again by generations of subsequent visitors — perceptiveness, diligence and fortitude, pride and dignity, curiosity and courtesy, literacy and a partiality for the martial arts, delicate beauty and a keen sense of social status.

After a decade in Japan William Adams would be quite ready to add some observations of his own: 'The people of this island of Japan are good of nature, courteous above measure and valiant in war: their justice is severely executed without any partiality upon transgressors of the law. They are governed in great civility. I mean, not a land better governed in the world by civil policy.'

This last was a recent development and largely the outcome of the efforts of one man, Tokugawa Ieyasu. Before Ieyasu's rise to power at the turn of the sixteenth century Japan had endured long years of torment. Sir George Sansom, that most respected of historians, quotes Tacitus to describe the character of the two centuries before the establishment of the Tokugawa regime: 'rich in disasters, dreadful in its battles, rent by its seditions and cruel even in its peace'.

When William Adams and his companions landed in Japan they found a country in the grip of civil war. In the eight-hundred-year-old capital city of Kyoto there lived a sacred emperor, at once both central to the existence of the state and irrelevant to the task of its daily governance. Like his predecessors for half a millennium he was no more than a puppet, preoccupied with religious rituals and the arts. Real power had for centuries been wielded by the *sei-i-tai shogun* — the 'barbarian-conquering generalissimo' — whose military dictatorship was blessed by the approval of the emperor. But for more than a century before Adams's arrival the power of the shogunate, nominally in the hands of the Ashikaga family, had been virtually nil as clan fought clan, reducing the country to a state of anarchy.

In the second half of the sixteenth century order and unity were gradually restored by three great warriors. Oda Nobunaga (1534–82) had established a firm power-base in central Japan until treacherously attacked and wounded by one of his own vassals. Accepting the hopelessness of his situation he took his own life by firing the temple in which he had taken refuge.

It was Nobunaga who had conceived the idea of reuniting Japan and who adopted the blunt slogan 'all the country under one sword'. It was his leading general, Toyotomi Hideyoshi (1536–98), who was to make this dream a reality. An ugly, ferocious little man, risen from the ranks, Hideyoshi proved himself not only a superb commander but also a statesman of towering ambition. Having brought the major part of the country under his control he launched a massive invasion of Korea, apparently intended as the first step towards the conquest of China and then of the whole world. His sudden death, however, cut short this dreadful and bloody enterprise and gave the long-awaited opportunity to Ieyasu, a trusted ally to whom the joint guardianship of Hideyoshi's chosen heir, Hideyori, had been given.

Ieyasu had been trained in a hard school. Thirteen years of his childhood and youth were passed in captivity as a hostage at the courts of rival clans. Such early experiences might well make a man into what Ieyasu became — watchful, devious, patient and ruthless. Something of the character of the man is revealed in the maxims attributed to him: 'Man's life is like going a long journey under a heavy burden: one must not hurry'. 'If you regard discomfort as a normal condition you are not likely to be troubled by want.' 'Consider anger as an enemy.' 'Let everyone realize his limitations. It is the biggest dew-drop that falls first from the leaf.'

Ieyasu, after Hideyoshi's death, found himself in an awkward position. As one of five regents he was sworn to ensure the succession of Hideyori. But, as the wealthiest and most powerful landholder in Japan, he also excited the envy of his fellow regents. Hideyori being an infant of five, the precarious stalemate which preserved his right to the succession could scarcely be expected to last until his maturity. The situation might reasonably have been expected to develop in one of two ways — a decisive resolution of the conflict between Ieyasu and his rivals or a general relapse into civil disorder. The past pattern of Japanese history seemed to suggest that the latter was more likely.

There was another potential source of instability in the realm at this time, a source not native but alien: the Christian religion and its professional representatives, Portuguese Jesuits and Spanish Franciscans. Europeans had first come to Japan more or less by accident. The traders, bringing guns, were quickly followed by priests, bringing the gospel. The Japanese seem to have seized hold of both with eager curiosity. St. Francis Xavier, pronouncing the Japanese 'the best people yet discovered', praised their rationality and inquisitiveness and proclaimed them 'the delight of my heart'. In the absence of any strong central government the Jesuits were relatively free to spread their doctrines and gained much encouragement from Japanese nobles who saw conversion as a

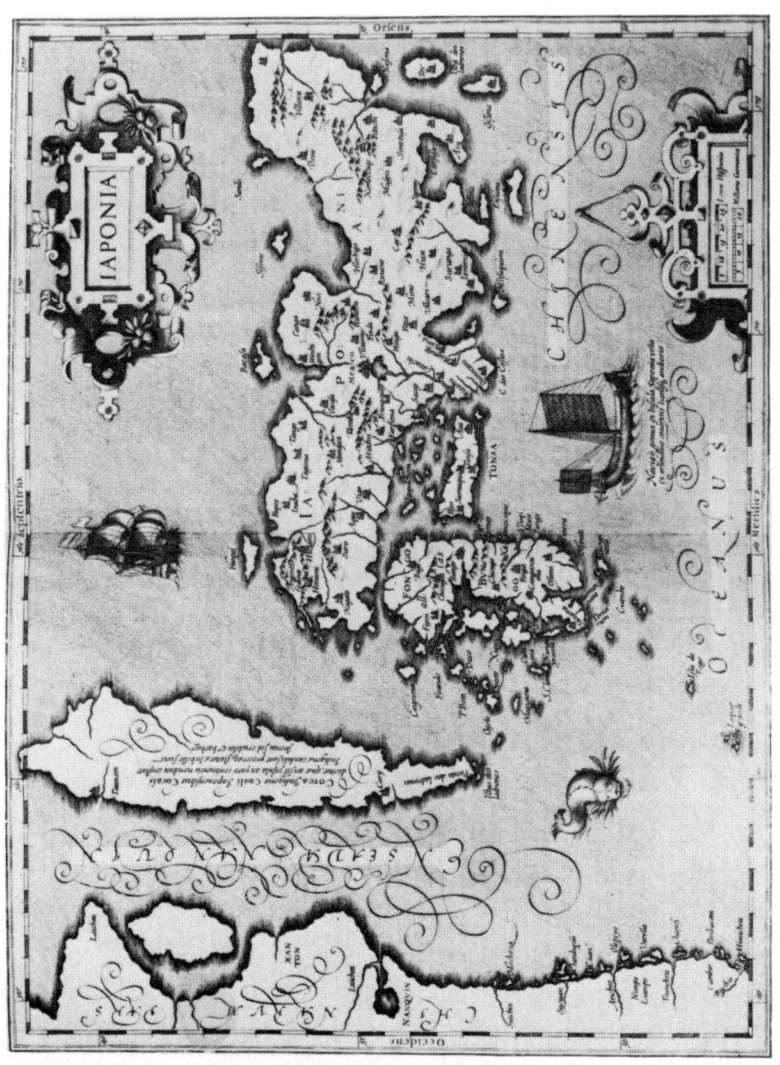

A seventeenth century map of Japan showing two islands at the tip of Korea and east of Kyushu named as 'ladrones' or robbers — piracy being a major problem during this period. Japan's northern island of Hokkaido is not included and the Korean peninsular is depicted as an island.

pathway to profitable trading opportunities. By 1582, the year of Nobunaga's death, it is estimated that there were some 150,000 Japanese converts; by the end of the century there was perhaps double that number.

In many ways the Christian newcomers enjoyed a privileged position. Nobunaga had welcomed them as a counterweight to the influence of the militant Buddhist sects. Numerous churches had been built and the newly established trading port of Nagasaki in the south-west was completely under Jesuit control. Success, however, seldom fails to arouse feelings of fear and envy. No less a man than Hideyoshi became uneasy at the power of the Christians, especially in the newly subordinated island of Kyushu. It seemed entirely possible that Christianized nobles, disgruntled at his ascendancy over them, might call in the aid of Christians from abroad to help them reassert their independence and thus destroy the peace he had so painfully established. In 1587, therefore, Hideyoshi suddenly ordered all his vassals to seek his permission before embracing the new religion and ordered all missionaries banished from Japan. But the order was not rigorously enforced. The arrival of the Spanish Franciscans and their quarrels with the Portuguese Jesuits deepened his dislike of the alien creed. In 1597 he abruptly ordered the crucifixion of nine missionaries and seventeen Japanese converts. It was a portent. But it was not heeded.

4

'The principal king'

'Our ship was brought into a good harbour, there to abide till the principal king of the whole island had news of us.'
LETTER OF WILLIAM ADAMS TO HIS WIFE, 1611

Visitors to Japan have often remarked upon the scrupulous honesty of the people. They have also noted their insatiable curiosity. In the case of Adams and his shipmates curiosity appears to have won the upper hand: 'many barks came aboard us. . . . The people offered us no hurt, but stole all things they could steal'.

On the following day the local *daimyo* — feudal overlord — 'sent soldiers aboard to see that none of the merchant's goods were stolen'. He also put a house at the disposal of the newcomers and laid on plentiful provisions. But three of the *Liefde*'s crew died within hours of landing and three more after a lingering period of illness. Meanwhile the ship was moved to a better harbour and word was sent to 'the principal king'.

Before any reply was received from Ieyasu, Adams and his companions found themselves subject to the interrogations of 'a Portugal Jesuit, with other Portugals' brought from the trading port of Nagasaki, which was virtually a Portuguese colony. The *Liefde* was a Dutch ship and Portugal was the enemy of the Netherlands on two grounds — that the Dutch, being Protestants, were heretics, and that as they resisted by force the right of the king of Spain to rule them (Portugal having been absorbed into the kingdom of Spain in 1580) they were rebels also. They therefore declared that the strangers were by no means merchants but pirates and, therefore, deserving of immediate execution, which in Japan meant an excruciatingly painful form of crucifixion. This fate seemed the more assured when two of the *Liefde*'s crew, to save their own lives, swore that they were the rightful owners of the ship's cargo and had been robbed by the rest of the crew, who by this act had proved themselves pirates indeed.

Portrait of Tokugawa Ieyasu.

No action was taken, however, until a summons was received from Ieyasu. Adams, accompanied by a single companion — 'commending myself into His hands that had preserved me from so many perils on the sea... was carried in one of the king's* galleys to the court at Osaka... about eighty leagues from where the ship was'.

On 12 May, a month and a day after reaching Japan, Adams was admitted to the presence of Tokugawa Ieyasu, his court being held in 'a wonderful costly house, gilded with gold in abundance'. After a period in which 'he made many signs unto me, some of which I understood and some I did not', a Portuguese interpreter was sent for. Ieyasu's keen interest in the world beyond his shores is evident in Adams's account of their interview:

'the king [here Ieyasu is called the 'king'; elsewhere he is called the 'emperor'] demanded of me, of what land I was, and what moved us to come to his land, being far off. I showed unto him the name of our country, and that our land had long sought out the East Indies, and desired friendship with all kings and potentates in way of merchandise, having in our land divers commodities which these lands had not; and also to buy such merchandise in this land, which our country had not. Then he asked whether our country had wars? I answered him yea, with the Spaniards and Portugals. He asked me in what did I believe? I said, in God, that made heaven and earth. He asked me divers other questions of things of my religion, and many other things — as what way we came to the country. Having a chart of the whole world I showed him, through the Strait of Magellan. At which he wondered and thought me to lie. Thus, from one thing to another, I abode with him till midnight. And having asked me what merchandise we had in our ship I showed him all. In the end, he being ready to depart, I desired that we might have trade of merchandise, as the Portugals and Spaniards had. To which he made me an answer, but what it was, I did not understand. So he commanded me to be carried to prison...'

Ieyasu's keen intelligence was motivated by his belief that

---

*In these accounts the Japanese rulers are regularly given European titles. Here, Ieyasu is 'king'. Elsewhere reference will be made to Ieyasu as 'emperor', although the real, ceremonial emperor lived in Kyoto and never met with the merchants. Ieyasu's son, Hidetada, is likewise called 'prince', 'king' and, occasionally, 'emperor'.

knowledge and ideas had real practical value; as an official chronicle of his reign took pains to stress:

'Having lived from boyhood to manhood in military encampments ... His Lordship had little time to read or study. Although he had conquered the country on horseback, being a man ... of wisdom, he fully appreciated the impossibility of governing the country on horseback. According to his judgement there could be no other way to govern the country than by a constant and deep faith in the sages and scholars, and as a human being interested in the welfare of his fellow human beings, he patronized scholarship from the very beginning of his rule.... Whatever the subject, he was interested, not in the turn of a phrase or in literary embellishments, but only in discovering the key to government — how to govern oneself, the people and the country.'

But Ieyasu's curiosity also had a more immediate objective. The cargo of the *Liefde* included a large quantity of arms and munitions: 500 matchlocks, 5,000 cannonballs, 300 chain-shot, 5,000 pound of gunpowder and 350 arrows. The Portuguese argued that a ship carrying such a load of armaments could scarcely be a peaceful trader. Ieyasu, however, was less concerned about the motives of the foreigners than the possibilities of securing the cargo they carried. If it fell into the hands of a rival his own position would be greatly endangered; if he secured it for his own use he might be able to establish his supremacy for good. He gave orders, therefore, that the *Liefde* should be brought to Osaka, and, after two days, Adams was sent for again and his interrogation repeated.

Adams was then 'commanded to prison again, but my lodging was bettered in an other place'. After thirty-nine days, hearing no news of his comrades, fearing 'every day to die' and knowing that 'the Jesuits and the Portugals gave many evidences against me and the rest', Adams was released. Ieyasu evidently cared little for European rivalries: 'the emperor [i.e. Ieyasu] gave them answer that we as yet had not done to him nor to none of his land any harm or damage; therefore, against reason and justice to put us to death. If our countries had wars the one with the other, that was no cause that he should put us to death.'

Adams found the captain, named Quaeckernaeck, and surviving crew in good health, 'and when I came aboard with weeping eyes was received; for it was given them to understand that I was executed long since. Thus, God be praised, all we that were left alive, came together again.'

From his companions, however, Adams discovered the extent of their losses; 'from the ship all things were taken out: so that the clothes that I took with me on my back I only had.' More important — a devastating blow to a pilot — 'all my instruments and books were taken.' It was small compensation that all 'unknown was to the emperor'. Immediate restitution was ordered, 'but it was here and there so taken, that we could not get it again'. Some 50,000 reals (Spanish dollars) in cash was made over to the use of the *Liefde*'s crew, to be disbursed through a Japanese official for their maintenance.

The *Liefde* having been moved, after a slow voyage against opposing winds, from Osaka to Edo, Ieyasu's capital (and today the city of Tokyo), much of the ship's company's new-found wealth was expended in trying to bribe various officials to secure permission for them to trade and depart. Treasure spent this way was spent in vain. Ieyasu meanwhile contemplated the turning-point of his career.

5
'Tighten the strings'

'After victory, tighten the strings of your helmet.'
JAPANESE PROVERB ATTRIBUTED TO TOKUGAWA IEYASU

The chief opposition to Ieyasu came not directly from his fellow regents but from an ambitious official, Ishida Mitsunari, who had enjoyed rapid advancement under Hideyoshi and sought to consolidate his power by playing on the fears of the great warlords who shared uneasily the tenuous authority he had bequeathed. By May 1600, the month in which Ieyasu, ostensibly visiting Hideyori in his massive stronghold of Osaka Castle, was questioning William Adams on his adventures and intentions, Ishida had built up a formidable alliance. These included three of the council of regents, Mori Terumoto and Uesugi Kagekatsu, the two wealthiest landowners after Ieyasu himself, and Ukita Hideie, the former commander-in-chief of Hideyoshi's Korean expeditionary force. Mori dominated the Inland Sea from his castle at Hiroshima while Uesugi held vast domains in the north of Honshu. Ieyasu, as a general of great reputation, was, however, able to win the allegiance of many of Hideyoshi's most famous captains. Each side also tended to draw supporters from the area around its central power-base — Ishida's being largely from the west, Ieyasu's from the east.

In the spring of the year 1600 intelligence reached Ieyasu that Uesugi was building extensive new fortifications in his northern stronghold. Ieyasu invited his fellow regent to explain his activities. He received a reply that was both pointed and insulting — city samurai might like to collect tea-ceremony bowls, but out in the country men tended to collect weapons. Ieyasu, however, declined to be drawn, suspecting that if he moved north-east against Uesugi, Ishida and his allies would seize Osaka while he was thus distracted. He did, however, give Ishida the impression that he was indeed planning to move against Uesugi, leaving Osaka on 26 July,

A contemporary drawing of the battle of Osaka in 1615. Osaka castle is top centre; the Tokugawa forces are featured coming from the east while the Toyotomi forces that were conquered are in the west.

reaching his own stronghold at Edo, after a leisurely journey, on 10 August, and then moving on to the north.

Ishida took the bait and on 27 August launched a furious assault on Fushimi Castle, which commanded the southern approaches to Kyoto. For ten days the garrison, commanded by Torii Mototada, one of Ieyasu's oldest and most trusted friends, resisted the onslaught. Even when a traitor, whose wife and children had been threatened with crucifixion by Ishida, set fire to a tower, Torii rejected a suggestion of glorious suicide. The objective of resistance, he insisted, was not personal honour but the strategic delay of Ishida's forces while Ieyasu gathered his strength. But he did lead his last 200 samurai in a gallant charge out of the gate to bring the fight to the enemy. After five such sorties the besieged garrison was reduced to 10 men. Torii, retiring into the castle, finally yielded to the demands of honour and committed suicide. The taking of Fushimi had cost Ishida 3,000 men.

The decisive confrontation between Ishida and Ieyasu took place at the little village of Sekigahara, some fifty miles to the north-east. The opposing armies manoeuvred into position in driving rain on the night of 20/21 October 1600. At dawn the whole area was blanketed in dense fog. Ishida's 80,000 troops were disposed to block the route westward, taking up their position beyond Sekigahara on the Nakasendo road and the hills either side of it, with Ishida's headquarters on the extreme left of the army. Ieyasu's slightly smaller force began to march towards the village at three in the morning and drew up their battle lines at about seven. Somewhere on the road behind him was Hidetada, his heir, with 38,000 men, but Ieyasu could delay no longer. Wearing armour but no helmet, he made a short speech to his commanders, concluding with the observation that there were only two ways to come back from the battlefield — with the head of an enemy or without your own. Ieyasu knew that he had to make a frontal assault on his enemies, who were in a strong position. He also knew that the command structure of their hastily assembled forces was weak and that defections in the course of the coming engagement were by no means unlikely. If they came they would certainly prove critical, for Hidetada's reinforcements were still nowhere in sight.

At eight o'clock the fog suddenly lifted. The first thrust of Ieyasu's forces was made against Ishida's centre, the charge soon losing its impetus and degenerating into a muddy morass of hand-to-hand combats. Meanwhile the main weight of Ieyasu's army was thrown against Ishida's contingent and command post. Hard-pressed, Ishida signalled for Kobayakawa Hideaki, stationed on the hills far away to the right, to commit his contingent to battle. After a delay in which Ishida's signals grew more and more frantic he at last did so — against Ishida's own centre. Ieyasu took immediate advantage of this act of treachery to order a general attack along the whole line of battle. At first it seemed that Ishida's centre might hold, but the defection of a second contingent on the extreme right broke their determination and they retired in total disarray. Ishida himself followed shortly afterwards.

By two in the afternoon Ieyasu was certain of victory. Sitting on his camp stool, he at last put on his helmet with great deliberation, remarking as he twisted the cords securely round the face-mask, 'after a victory tighten the strings of your helmet'. Those who knew him well at once caught the meaning of this enigmatic utterance — prudence is even more necessary when one is tempted to give way to exultation in success. But Ieyasu did allow himself the traditional pleasure of viewing the heads of his enemies.

Sekigahara was a dramatic victory but it was not entirely a decisive one. Ishida had been smashed but Hideyori was still alive and still the heir. Ieyasu would have to move carefully to make the most of his new position. And carefully but relentlessly he began to reorganize the political map of Japan. Of the eighty-seven daimyo who had opposed him at Sekigahara all but six lost their lives or their lands or their freedom. Those who had been loyal to the Tokugawa cause were rewarded with enlarged holdings, generally close to the Tokugawa domains. Opponents and waverers, those who kept their estates, were designated *tozama* — 'outer lords' — condemned quite literally to exist on the periphery of the realm.

Mori Terumoto, the regent currently in charge of Hideyori, had taken no part in the battle and, seeing the chance of preserving his domains, allowed Ieyasu to enter Osaka Castle on 1 November. Mori and Uesugi nevertheless suffered a severe reduction in the amount of their holdings. Ieyasu meanwhile took control of the country's chief mines, forests, harbours and markets. In 1603 he secured for himself the office of shogun, to which Nobunaga and even Hideyoshi had not dared to aspire. But he took pains to avoid the appearance of disputing the position of Hideyori, knowing well that there were still generals who would rise in his defence. At Edo he built an immense fortress, but took care to reside elsewhere. At Kyoto he built a new residence, Nijo Castle, and installed a deputy to keep an eye on the emperor's court. He also strengthened the garrisons in the fortresses which surrounded the imperial city. In 1605 he resigned the title of shogun in favour of his heir, Hidetada, and went to live in prudently fortified luxury at Suruga, on the sea-coast south-west of Edo. This released him from various ceremonial duties and enabled him to continue to wield real power from the seclusion of apparent retirement.

6

'grace and favour'

'Now being in such grace and favour . . . I pleased him so, that what I said he would not contrary.'
LETTER OF WILLIAM ADAMS, 22 OCTOBER 1611

While Ieyasu was thus inexorably securing the fortunes of his dynasty Adams and his companions were still rather less effectually attempting to negotiate their release, 'in which suit we spent much of the money given us'.

After many frustrating months, all efforts proving vain, Adams and his shipmates came to a parting of the ways:

'three or four of our men rebelled against the captain and myself, and made a mutiny with the rest of our men, so that we had much trouble with them. For they would not abide no longer in the ship, but everyone would be a commander: and perforce would have every part of the money that was given by the emperor. . . . In the end, the money was divided according to every man's place; but this was about two years that we had been in Japan; and when we had a denial that we should not have our ship, but to abide in Japan.'

Having divided up their remaining capital 'every one took his way where he thought best'. Ieyasu's further generosity cushioned them from the risk of destitution: 'the emperor gave every man, to live upon, two pounds of rice a day, daily, and yearly so much as was worth eleven or twelve ducats a year . . . myself, the captain and mariners all alike.' No doubt this munificence was in part motivated by Ieyasu's desire to prevent the men from turning to theft to keep themselves alive.

Adams was soon singled out for special treatment on account of his extraordinary talents and abilities. Ieyasu, eager to take every advantage of western technology and duly impressed by the pilot's fantastic voyage, commanded him to build a ship like the one that had carried him so far. 'I answered that I was no carpenter and had no knowledge thereof. Well, do your endeavour, saith he: if it be not good, it is no matter.' Adams built the ship. It was roughly half the size of the *Liefde*, 'about eighty tons burden or thereabout'. It was certainly what the shogun had hoped for, 'being made in all respects as our manner is', and 'he coming aboard to see it, liked it very well'.

The pilot served not merely as a handyman but as a tutor also and Ieyasu proved an earnest pupil of 'geometry and ... the art of mathematics'. His gratitude was shown by the easy access granted to his person 'so that I came often in his presence' and also by his generosity, giving Adams presents 'from time to time' and raising his yearly stipend to 'much about seventy ducats by the year'.

As a result of Adams's intimacy and influence with Ieyasu his 'former enemies did wonder' and the 'Jesuits and Portugals ... entreated me to befriend them to the emperor in their business; and so by my means both Spaniards and Portugals ... received friendship from the emperor, I recompensing their evil unto me with good'. But the Portuguese were not content to rely upon Adams's goodwill and attempted to bring him firmly under their control by converting him to the Catholic faith. A Jesuit father from Nagasaki was chosen for the task. The following account of his efforts is written from the Portuguese point of view:

'The father spoke to the chief of them [i.e. Adams] and offered to procure for him and his companions a safe-conduct permitting them to leave Japan. The father was afraid lest they should contaminate, with their conversation and perverse doctrines, the souls of the Christians, still fresh and tender in the Catholic faith. But the Englishman did not accept the offer, alleging that for many reasons the king would not willingly give them such permission. However he thanked the father, who took advantage of the occasion to demonstrate to him the falsity of his sect, and the truth of the Catholic religion, by arguments and obvious reasons, drawn from the Holy Bible. But he wasted his time with the obstinate heretic, who had a lively intelligence and, though he had not studied, tried to justify his errors by citing the authority of the same holy scriptures which, however, he misunderstood and misinterpreted. And although he ought to have been convinced by the force and truth of the reasons advanced by the father, he persisted in his obstinacy.'

To forgive the Jesuits for trying to have him crucified was one thing for Adams, to forget quite another.

The pilot's advancement may have appalled his enemies but it brought him no nearer freedom. 'In the end of five years I made supplication to the king to go out of this land, desiring to see my poor wife and children according to conscience and nature. With the which request the emperor was not well pleased and would not let me go any more for my country, but to bide in his land.' Persistence brought the shogun's favourite no reward: 'in process of time, being in great favour with the emperor, I made supplication again, by reason we had news the Hollanders were in ... Patania [i.e. Patani, in Siam]: which rejoiced us much, with hope that God should bring us to our country again, by one means or other. So I made supplication again and boldly spoke myself with him, at which he gave me no answer.'

Adams then tried appealing to Ieyasu's self-interest, rather than his sense of gratitude or compassion, 'I told him, if he would permit me to depart, I would be a means that both the English and Hollanders should come and traffic there'. All to no avail — 'by no means he would let me go'. Ieyasu did, however, see a way to have his cake and eat it. 'He answered, that he was desirous of both these nations' company for traffic, but would not part with me ... but bade me write to that purpose.'

Eventually a concession was granted — but not to Adams. 'I asked him leave for the captain the which he presently granted me. So by that means my captain got leave; and in a Japan junk sailed to Pattan.' Adams learned only some years later of Quaeckernaeck's fate: 'in a year's space came no Hollanders. In the end he went from Patane to Ior, where he found a fleet of nine sail; of which fleet Matleef was General: and in this fleet he was made master again, which fleet sailed to Malacca, and fought with an armada of Portugals; in which battle he was shot and presently died.' Adams's old shipmate Melchior van Santvoort, who accompanied him, did, however, return safely to Japan.

As the shogun's trusted aide, the pilot continued to prosper. After acquiring a considerable estate at Hemi, forty miles south of Edo near Uraga Bay, Adams informed his 'unknown countrymen' in a letter written in October 1611 that 'for my services which I have done and daily do, being employed in the emperor's service, he hath given me a living, like unto a lordship in England, with eighty or ninety husbandmen, that be as my slaves or servants; which, or the like precedent, was never here before given to any stranger. Thus God have provided for me after my great misery.'

Resigned to his fate, Adams decided to marry a Japanese lady, Magome Kageyu. It was almost certainly a love-match, for her father was a minor government official of no great wealth or rank. Adams's Japanese wife was to bear him two children, Joseph and

Susanna, and to remain his devoted companion until his death. As a man of some standing and property Adams also found himself able to set up in business on his own account. He therefore bought a house in Edo's Nihonbashi district. A Japanese samurai could never have had anything to do with trade. But Adams was a foreigner. And foreigners were different. So there were some advantages in having a status that was as ambiguous as it was exalted.

7

'the governor of Manilia'

'A great ship of 1,000 tons, which came from Manilia . . . was cast away upon this coast, where in was the governor of Manilia.'
LETTER OF WILLIAM ADAMS, DECEMBER 1613

Adams's antipathy to the Spanish and Portuguese may be attributed to the prejudices normal to a Protestant Englishman of the period, confirmed no doubt by their efforts to have him crucified upon his arrival in Japan. But it may also reasonably be attributed to his continuing experience of their arrogance and enmity towards him.

Spanish activity in Japan was greatly stimulated in 1608 when the pope deprived the Portuguese Jesuits of their monopoly of missionary work in Japan and thus opened the way to the incursion of dozens of Spanish Franciscans who sought to compensate with zeal for what they lacked in local knowledge and understanding.

In the same year Ieyasu sent Adams on a commercial embassy to the Philippines, hoping to persuade the Spanish colonial authorities to open up direct trade with Japan. Adams gained an audience with the governor, Don Rodrigo Vivero y Velasco, a Mexican-born favourite of Anne, the consort of Philip II of Spain, and, therefore, a gentleman of the highest rank. Adams's mission must be reckoned a success, for the governor sent him back to Japan with letters and presents for the shogun and instructions to deliver them in person. Thereafter a regular trade was opened by means of the galleon which sailed between Manila and New Spain (Mexico).

The year following his mission to the Philippines Adams renewed his acquaintance with Don Rodrigo under circumstances distinctly more uncomfortable to that distinguished grandee. 'In the year 1609 was cast away a great ship called the *San Francisco* . . . upon the coast of Japan, in the latitude of 35 degrees and 50 minutes. By distress of weather she cut overboard her main-mast and bore up for Japan, and in the night unawares, the ship ran upon the shore and was cast away: in the which thirty and six men were drowned, and three hundred forty, or three hundred fifty saved: in which ship the Governor of Manila as a passenger was to return to Nova Spania.'

Don Rodrigo had, upon his appointment as governor and captain-general of the Philippines, shown great kindness to a group of two hundred Japanese whom he found in captivity, liberated and sent home. Ieyasu was apparently delighted to have the opportunity to repay this benevolence in kind, and throughout his enforced sojourn in Japan the shipwrecked Spaniard was treated with the greatest respect and generosity. His account of his experiences is worthy of extensive quotation, for he describes people and places that Adams most certainly would have known but of which he has left us no description in his own words and which had by this time perhaps become so familiar to him that he could not have captured their most distinctive features with the freshness and immediacy of the newly arrived traveller. He also comments at length on the manners and customs of the Japanese; the drunkenness of the men and the fidelity of the women, the zeal of public officials and the pride of the nobles, all find a place in his observations.

In the immediate aftermath of their shipwreck the Spanish found succour in a nearby village whose inhabitants readily gave them food and shelter. Within a few days the local lord arrived in state, accompanied by three hundred armed retainers. Treating Don Rodrigo with the greatest deference, he gave him presents and announced his intention of paying the expenses of the entire ship's company while they were in his domain. A month later they were conveyed to Edo, where Hidetada kept court.

The governor of Manila, by no means an unsophisticated man, was greatly impressed by many aspects of the city: the cheapness of the food, the comfort of the houses, the efficiency of the police and the cleanliness of the streets, these last 'so ... well kept, that it might be imagined no person walked in them'. The city was also apparently impressed by the visitors: for a week after their arrival the Spaniards were pestered by curious onlookers until a guard was placed outside their lodging and a placard, signed by a magistrate, set up to prohibit further interference with their privacy.

If Don Rodrigo was impressed by the city, he was astonished by the court which lay at its heart. In his account of his audience he plainly declares that 'I should think myself fortunate if I could succeed in affording an exact idea of all the wonders I saw there, as well in respect to the material of the buildings at this royal residence, as to the pomp and splendour of the court. I think I may affirm, that from the entrance to the prince's [i.e. Hidetada's] apartment, there were more than 20,000 persons, not assembled for the occasion, but constantly employed and paid for the daily service of the courts.'

To reach Hidetada's presence chamber the visitors had to pass through the immense outer walls of Edo Castle, across its deep moat, through a complex system of drawbridges, gates and inner walls, all lined with hundreds of armed men, and past a huge stables and arsenal. 'Next we came to the first apartment of the palace.... The walls and ceiling are covered with wooden panelling and decorated with various paintings of hunting scenes, done in gold, silver and other colours, so that the wood itself is not visible. Although in our opinion this first compartment left nothing to be desired, the second chamber was finer, while the third was even more splendid; and the further we proceeded, the greater the wealth and novelty that met our eyes.'

Hidetada is described as being in his middle thirties, dark, good-looking and well-built. Although the visitor was seated in a place of honour, four paces to the left of the shogun, and the conversation was largely confined to courteous pleasantries, Hidetada could not apparently resist giving him a lesson in gentlemanly behaviour. 'He told me to cover my head and then smiled, saying to the interpreters that for all he had desired to meet and know me, it grieved him to think I should be sad over my loss. Men of position, he continued, should not grieve over enterprises which had turned out badly: such things were not their fault and I should, therefore rejoice, for he would grant me everything I desired while in his kingdom. I thanked him for his kindness and answered him as best I could.'

Four days after this interview, Don Rodrigo set off to visit Ieyasu at Suruga. The density of population of the countryside through which he passed continued to amaze him — 'on whichever side the traveller turns his eye, he sees a crowd of people passing to and fro, as though he were in the most populous cities of Europe.' Exhilirated by the prospect about him, the honoured guest confided to his diary that 'if he could have prevailed upon himself to renounce his God and his king, he should have preferred that country to his own.'

A week after arriving in Suruga, having been handsomely lodged and once again pestered by the local inhabitants, Don Rodrigo was conducted to Ieyasu's residence. This struck him as rather smaller than Hidetada's, but even more splendid in its appointments. Before entering the former shogun's presence, the visitor was briefed by a court official who congratulated him on the signal honour he was about to receive in being permitted to look the most powerful man in Japan straight in the face. He was warned that a foreigner might find the formality with which he would be received rather cold and unwelcoming, but he should know that a Japanese noble would esteem himself fortunate in being allowed to look at Ieyasu from a distance of a hundred paces, lying face down on the floor. The Spaniard, in no way discountenanced, calmly replied that as King Philip of Spain was the greatest and most powerful sovereign in the universe, and as he came as his representative, no distinction that could be conferred upon him would be too great. The court official was simply stunned by this response and, having slapped his forehead with the palm of his hand in token of his astonishment, retired in hasty confusion to consult with Ieyasu. Half an hour later he reappeared to inform Don Rodrigo that he would be honoured in an unprecedented manner which would be the talk of the entire country.

Despite his haughty manner, the visitor, no stranger to court ceremonial, was greatly confounded by the sumptuousness and dignity of his audience:

'I followed the minister, who conducted me into the presence of the sovereign, who I saluted. He was in a kind of square box, not very large, but remarkably rich. It was raised two steps above the floor and surrounded, at four paces distance, by a gold lattice-work six feet high, in which were small doors by which the emperor's attendants went in and out, as they were called from the crowd, on their hands and knees.... The monarch was encircled by nearly twenty grandees, ministers, or principle courtiers, in long silk robes and trousers ... so long that they entirely concealed the feet. The emperor was seated upon a kind of stool, of blue satin worked with stars and half-moons of silver. In his girdle he wore a sword and had his hair bound up with ribbons of different colours, but had no other head-dress. His age appeared to be about sixty; he was of middling height and very stout. His face was dignified and gracious.'

After a brief exchange of courtesies Don Rodrigo attempted to retire but was requested to remain seated while a visiting lord was admitted to the august presence. The noble brought bars of gold and silver and bales of silk, which the Spaniard estimated to be worth 20,000 ducats and which Ieyasu did not even bother to

An early seventeenth century Dutch print of the Shogun's court at Yedo (Tokyo).

acknowledge. A hundred paces from the throne the daimyo threw himself full length on the ground and, having remained thus prostrate for several minutes, retired with his suite of some 3,000 attendants. Throughout the presentation not a word was spoken. After further similar introductions Don Rodrigo was escorted from the palace with great ceremony, having been invited to pass to the former shogun any requests he might care to make.

Not in the least abashed by the implications of the charade which he had witnessed, the Spaniard submitted three requests — that Christian priests should be granted royal protection and freedom of movement, that friendship might continue between the ruler of Japan and the King of Spain and that, as evidence of that friendship, the ruler of Japan should drive the Dutch from his domains. Ieyasu's reply was a model of diplomatic tact and self-possession. Commending the Spaniard on asking nothing for himself, though destitute, but only for his religion and his king, Ieyasu granted the first two requests but declined to expel the Dutch — who had just been granted trading rights — on the grounds that he was bound by his word of honour to let them remain in Japan for a year. Nevertheless he thanked his visitor for warning against their rebellions and piratical tendencies. He then informed Don Rodrigo that a ship would be placed at his disposal to enable him to continue his journey to New Spain. In return he requested the services of fifty miners from that mineral-rich colony to enable him to make more productive use of Japan's own silver mines.

Leaving Suruga to make their way to Kyushu, where they were due to take ship, Don Rodrigo's party passed through Kyoto, a city whose immensity made Edo as nothing in comparison. 'I learnt that the city has a population of over 800,000 people, while according to different estimates between 300,000 and 400,000 folk lived in the vicinity. At any rate it is certainly true that there is no larger place in the known world'. Staggered by the impact of this metropolis, the proud visitor took extra care to conceal his feelings 'lest they might think that Spain has nothing comparable'.

No less staggering than the size of the city (estimated at thirty miles in circumference) was the number of its monuments and amenities. 'the viceroy told me that . . . there were 5,000 temples of their gods, as well as many hermitages. He also said that there were some 50,000 registered public women placed by the authorities in special districts.' Of all the sights in or around the imperial capital, two in particular seemed to Rodrigo worthy of extended description. One was the fifty-three-foot-high 'Doubuton' (i.e. *Daibutsu*, or 'Great Buddha') at nearby Nara:

'This metal idol [the *Daibutsu*] might well be included among the seven wonders of the world and I fancy that it is comparable to the most wonderful of them all.... Wondering how I could describe it when I returned home, I told a servant belonging to the great nobles who were accompanying me to climb up and measure the thumb of the idol's right hand.... the fellow clambered up and tried to encircle the thumb with both his arms; but however much he stretched, he was unable to make his hands meet around the thumb.... its proportions are no less admirable for it is one of the most perfectly fashioned things that I have ever seen.'

The other sight that impressed was the tomb of Hideyoshi. With its lavish profusion of jasper, gold and silver, solemn chanting and silent crowds of pilgrims, it was similarly awesome but Rodrigo 'grieved... to think that the abominable purpose of such famous and magnificent buildings was the worship of the ashes of a man whose soul was in hell for all eternity.'

From Kyoto the party made its way to Osaka then on to the Portuguese trading post at Nagasaki. But the vessel assigned for the use of Don Rodrigo and his companions was soon found to be unseaworthy and so he accepted Ieyasu's invitation to return to Suruga until another ship could be put at his disposal. Taking advantage of renewed contact with the ex-shogun the Spaniard again tried to persuade him to expel the Dutch from his shores, but without success. Ironically, when he and his party did leave in August 1610, it was aboard a ship of 120 tons built by William Adams, probably with the assistance of the Dutch ship's carpenter from the *Liefde*. This ship carried the Spanish party safely to Acapulco and, in Adams's own words, 'in 1611 this Governor returned another ship in her room, with a great present, and with an Ambassador to the emperor, giving him thanks for his friendship: and also sent the worth of the emperor's ship in goods and money: which ship the Spaniards have now in the Philippines.'

The ambassador received by Ieyasu in 1611 was Sebastian Vizcaino, an experienced surveyor who had been charged to map the coastlines of Japan and to search for certain nearby islands reputed to be rich in gold and silver. Ieyasu granted permission when the Spanish asked to make a survey of the coasts, explaining that they wanted to ensure that future trading vessels would know where to find safe anchorage in the event of storms. He was, however, much less compliant when the Spaniards asked him yet again to drive the

Dutch from his lands.

Ieyasu replied stiffly that no foreign sovereign should presume to dictate to him how he should govern his dominions, that the quarrels between various European states were of no concern to him and that as long as strangers obeyed the laws and dealt honestly with his subjects it was a matter of indifference to him whether they were held to be rebels on the other side of the world. When the Spanish and Portuguese unwisely raised their request yet again in a joint petition Ieyasu finally cast aside self-restraint, driving their spokesmen from his presence and thundering after them that if 'the devils of hell' were to come to Japan they should be treated like 'angels from heaven' for as long as they were obedient to the laws. His policy, he declared in a calmer moment, was that the country should be 'an asylum for people of all nations. No man who has taken refuge in my dominions and conducts himself peaceably, shall be compelled, against his will, to abandon the empire.'

Vizcaino struck Ieyasu as arrogant to the point of insolence when he insisted on observing Spanish court etiquette and threatened to return to Mexico if he did not have his own way. Ieyasu, therefore, asked Adams if all Europeans were as insufferable as the Spaniards; Adams naturally assured him that they were not and indeed would certainly agree with Ieyasu that the self-regard of the Spaniards was quite excessive.

Exploiting the advantage Ieyasu had thus given him, Adams explained that the Spanish were bent on nothing less than the conquest of the entire world, not simply by force of arms but by the stealthy conversion of the subjects of foreign princes. Once a substantial minority had been converted by the Jesuits and other missionaries, an armed invasion would follow. The converts would side with their coreligionists and the overthrow of the established government and subjugation of non-Catholics would swiftly follow. This had happened in the Philippines and was the cause of the opposition of the Dutch and English to Spanish ambitions. In the light of this policy, Adams suggested, it might not have been altogether wise for Ieyasu to have allowed Vizcaino to make charts of the coast of Japan. Certainly no European monarch would have allowed an alien power so easily to acquire vital strategic information. Ieyasu took note of Adams's words but told him proudly that if any power tried to invade his realm its forces would be cut to pieces as they came ashore.

At it turned out Vizcaino gave a higher priority to gold-hunting than to surveying. There was no gold to be found and as the

Spanish had made themselves so obnoxious to the Japanese, when they were obliged to buy a ship for their return voyage they had to sell their very shirts and bedding to pay for it. They left Japan empty-handed in October 1613. Adams, despite his long-standing animosity towards the subjects of the Most Catholic King, must scarcely have noted their departure, because by that time, after an interval of fifteen years, he was once again united with his countrymen.

8

'discreet friend, Willem Adams'

'Honourable, dear and discreet friend Willem Adams.'
LETTER OF VICTOR SPRINCKEL, 6 FEBRUARY 1608

The letter inviting the Dutch to trade with Japan, which Adams had promoted but which Ieyasu had entrusted to Quaeckernaeck and van Santvoort, was handed over to the Dutch authorities at Patani in December 1605. It took a further two years for it to reach the Netherlands and for an expedition to be fitted out in response to the invitation. And it was not until a further eighteen months had passed that two Dutch vessels, the *Roode Leeuw met Pijlen* and the *Griffoen*, anchored off Nagasaki. Thus four years had passed between the departure of the two Dutchmen from Japan and the arrival of their countrymen eager to challenge the trading monopoly of their national enemies, the Spanish and Portuguese. But their arrival was not entirely unanticipated. In February 1608 Sprinckel, the chief Dutch merchant at Patani, had written to Adams in the most ingratiating terms, requesting him to pass on to the shogun a letter explaining that the failure of the Dutch to respond to his invitation to trade was due, not to lack of interest on their part, but to an acute shortage of shipping, the result of losses suffered in sea fights against the Portuguese.

Leaving Nagasaki after a few days, the two ships travelled north-west to the small port of Hirado, where they were welcomed by Adams, who immediately offered to help them negotiate trading privileges at the court of the shogun. Adams's inside knowledge was to prove invaluable. As a long-time resident he knew the language well. And as a courtier himself, he knew not only the acceptable forms of etiquette but also the niceties of protocol which attached to the tricky matter of present-giving. The Dutch were, according to Adams, 'in great friendship received' and Ieyasu granted them the right to trade in all Japanese ports and inland towns as well as giving them permission to establish a permanent trading post at Hirado. The organization of this task was placed in

View of the Dutch house at Hirado from an illustration published in 1670.

the hands of one Jacques Specx. Having accomplished their mission, the two Dutch ships sailed for Patani in October 1609.

A year passed without further contact. Specx, fearing some disaster, went to Patani to investigate and found that once again it was the chronic shortage of shipping which was delaying the development of regular trade. Upbraiding his colleagues for neglecting to exploit such a hard-won opportunity, Specx returned with a shipload of stock and sped off to Ieyasu's court to reassure him that the Dutch were seriously interested in commerce with Japan and to reconfirm the trading privileges granted two years earlier.

Once again Adams accompanied the Dutch merchants to court, serving both as interpreter and intermediary and offering them the hospitality of his house in Edo. Not only did he eventually manage to secure a renewal of the trading rights, he even managed to win them the privilege of carrying on their commercial activities entirely without the supervision of Japanese officials.

Specx's ship, bringing 'cloth, lead, elephants' teeth, damask, and black taffities, raw silk, pepper and other commodities' was 'wondrously well received' so that, in Adams's pungent phrase, 'the Hollanders have here an Indies of money'.

Adams was rewarded for his efforts at court with a present of bolts of cloth. So great was his value to the Dutch, indeed, that they not only rewarded him but long betrayed his trust as well. Desperate to get word to his family in England regarding his whereabouts and safety, and not unnaturally concerned to make contact with his own countrymen, he gave many letters into the safe-keeping of Dutch friends, begging them to pass them on as they could. His efforts at communication were for a long time deliberately frustrated as he noted himself in a letter to the English merchant Augustin Spalding in Bantam, Java, on 12 January 1613:

'Had I known our English ships had trade with the Indies, I had long ago troubled you with writing; but the Hollanders have kept it most secret from me till the year 1611, which was the first news that I heard of the trading of our ship in the Indies. . . . Your friendly and Christian letter I have received by the Hollanders which be here arrived this year 1612, by which I do understand that you have received my letter by Peter Johnssoon, of which I am very glad, hoping that my poor wife and friends shall hear I am alive. For unto this present there hath not come to the hands of my friends any letter of mine, being by the Hollanders intercepted always; for by the company of this ship I have certain news of truth that it is expressly forbid by the ... Indish Company that they shall carry nor bring any letters in no manner of ways; for by both these ships I have had divers letters sent me by my wife and other good friends out of England and Holland, but few came to my hand and those that I have received the most part were two letters which came from London by the conveyance of the *Globe* of London. These two letters have not been opened, but forty or fifty days detained from me.'

Nevertheless, Adams remained a firm and loyal friend to the Dutch until his dying day. That his friendship was worth having we can well imagine from his boast to Spalding that 'The Hollanders be now settled, and I have got them that privilege as the Spaniards and Portugals could never get in this fifty or sixty years in Japan.'

Indeed so eminent was Adams's position that 'It hath pleased God to bring things to pass, so as in the eyes of the world must seem strange: for the Spaniard and Portugal hath been my bitter enemies to death; and now they must seek to me, an unworthy wretch; for the Spaniard as well as the Portugal must have all their negotiations to through my hand. God have praise for it.' Adams evidently did not, however, feel inclined to take forgiveness to the point of undue exertion: 'This year 1612 the Spaniards and Portugals have used me as an instrument to get their liberty in the manner of the Hollands, but upon consideration of further inconvenience I have not sought it for them.'

9

'let them inquire for me'

'If it be that there come a ship near unto the easternmost part, let them inquire for me. I am called in the Japan tongue Anjin-sama.'
LETTER OF WILLIAM ADAMS TO AUGUSTIN SPALDING, 12 JANUARY 1613

Although Adams's attempts to communicate with England had been frustrated by the Dutch, they could not keep his existence and influence a secret forever. By 1611 the directors of the English East India Company had decided that the fleet to be sent to India that year should have as a secondary objective the opening of trade with Japan. They therefore specifically instructed its commander in his sailing instructions 'to consult and take good advice with the rest of the factors and especially with William Adams, an English man now resident there and in great favour with the king as we hear, to desire his opinion what course should be held'.

Adams, who had, after all, had more than a decade to reflect upon the question, had very decided views on 'what course should be held'. His letter of January 1613 to the English merchant Augustin Spalding in Bantam is full of commercial advice. Adams assures his correspondent that the English can be sure of a warm welcome, 'and this I do insure you of, for it is in my power to do it. I do praise God for it: who hath given me favour with the emperor, and good will to me, so far as that I may boldly say our countrymen shall be so welcome and free in comparison as in the river of London'.

He then turns briskly to the prospects for business. 'And now to the purpose. I fear that there will be no profit, which is principal: for the commodities of our country are here good cheap, that is cloth; for by reason of the ship that comes from Novo Spaynia of the one party and the Hollanders on the other party, hath made the price of cloth so good and cheap as in England. Eight or nine years ago cloth was very dear, but now very cheap.' Better, he therefore advises, to bring what the Dutch do — lead, steel, glassware, mirrors, amber, fancy textiles and spices. As for return of freights there are such commodities as rice, fish, bisquit and, thanks to the trade wars in the Moluccas, a lively traffic in munitions. Having warned of the uncertainties of the carrying trade with China — 'some years good cheap and some year dear' — Adams nevertheless urges that 'can our English merchants get the handling of trade with the Chinas, then shall our country make great profit'.

On the subject of tariffs, he was reassuring: 'the charges in Japan are not great: only a present for the emperor and a present for the king, and two or three other presents for the secretaries. Other customs here be none.'

As a pilot, Adams had naturally given much thought to the question of the best site for an initial anchorage and later for a possible trading-post: 'if a ship do come, let her come for the easterly part of Japan ... where the king and the emperor court is: for come our ships to Ferando [i.e. Hirado] where the Hollanders be, it is far to the court, about 230 leagues, a wearisome way and foul.... about this easterly part of the land there be the best harbours and a coast so clear as there is no shoals or rocks half a mile from the main land. It is good also for sale of merchandise and security for ships, for which case I have sent a pattron [pattern, i.e. chart] of Japan, for which myself I have been all about the coast in the shipping that I have made for the emperor....'

Adams then concludes his memorandum with an invitation to any English ship to ask for him by name (Anjin-sama: 'Lord Pilot') upon arrival — 'by that name am I known all the sea coast along' — and with a curiously repetitive assurance of his desire to do his best for the newcomers: 'and comes there a ship here, I hope the worshipful company shall find me to be a servant of your servants to serve them in such a manner as they shall be satisfied of my service.'

All this advice was to prove of little avail, being written only days before the English fleet left Bantam, Java, for Japan and, therefore, arriving long after its departure. In the event, the reunion between Adams and his countrymen was to give rise to misunderstandings and strained relations that neither side had bargained for.

When the English ship *Clove* finally entered the harbour at Hirado on 11 June 1613 Adams was far away in Edo. It was to be six weeks before the captain, John Saris, was to meet him. During that time he was to learn much about Japan.

No sooner had the *Clove* dropped anchor than she was visited by the local daimyo, Ho-in. An exchange of courtesies was followed by entertainment in Saris's cabin — 'a banquet ... and a

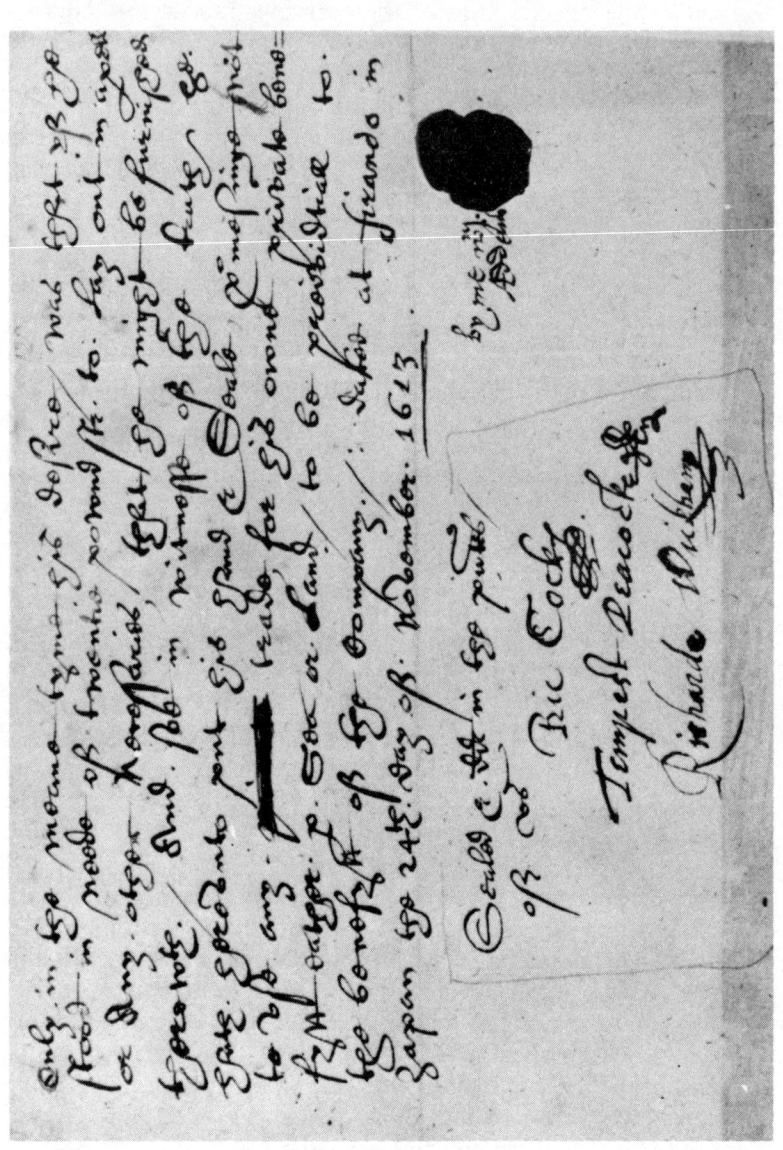

Will Adams' contract of employment with the East India Company.

good consort of music, which much delighted them'. Saris handed over a letter from King James, which his noble guest 'received with great joy' but put away until Adams came and could translate it for him. The departure of Ho-in was followed by the immediate arrival of 'all his nobility, attended with a multitude of soldiers.... We being pestered with the number of these visitors, I sent to the king, requesting him that order might be sent to a guardian with charge to remain and lie aboard, that no injury might be offered unto us; and caused a proclamation to be made in the town to the same effect.' Before nightfall another visitor had presented himself, Henrik Brouwer, successor to Specx as head of the Dutch factory at Hirado. Saris was sure he came 'to see what passed between the king [i.e. Ho-in] and us' but gave him supper nevertheless. He then completed the work of an eventful day by writing a note to Adams in Edo, advising him of the *Clove*'s arrival.

On the following day, the *Clove* having been towed much closer inshore, 'there came continually such a world of people aboard, both men and women, as we were not able to go upon the decks, and all about the ship was covered with boats full of people.' Saris allowed 'divers of the better sort of women' to come into his cabin, where, seeing a 'picture of venus... very lasciviously set out... they fell down and worshipped it', much to his astonishment. This seemingly extraordinary behaviour was soon explained 'in a whispering manner (that some of their own companions, which were not so, might not hear) that they were Christians, whereby we perceived them to be of the portingale-made papists'. 'Mr. Addams his host [i.e. the man Adams stayed with when he was in Hirado] came and brought me a letter, which he had left with him the last monsoon when he was here, to deliver from him to the first English ship arriving here... ordering a post to be sent for him overland, which I did, not withstanding I had formerly writ, which was by the king's means sent away with speed.'

Ho-in also came aboard again with four female companions who 'seemed to be somewhat bashful, but he willed them to be frolic'. Returning the compliment of the previous day, he commanded one of the ladies to give a recital on the shamisen which to Saris 'did much resemble our lute, being bellied like it, but longer in the neck, and fretted like ours, but had only four gut strings.... Their fingering with the left hand, like ours, very nimbly, but the right hand striketh with an ivory bone, as we use to play upon a cittern with a quill.'

On 13 June Saris and 'the merchants, the master and best of the sailors' went ashore with many gifts for Ho-in who feasted him in return and drank a pint and a half of saké straight off in honour of the King of England. Having followed this example, Saris still remembered somehow to send a quantity of 'Spanish wine and ... strong beer' to the Dutch as a present. The next two days were likewise occupied with judicious present-giving and on the 16th Saris took out a six-month lease on a house from Andrea Dittis, a Chinese-Christian trader. The acquisition of a shore base had come none too soon, for the crew were becoming restless; that night, the ship's baker 'was taken by the master, swimming ashore in the night, yet he and others pardoned at entreaty of friends' and the next day 'Fransisco, a swart [i.e. black] whipped at the mast for stealing John Japan's cloak'.

On 21 June Ho-in once more came aboard the *Clove* with some female company, this time proving not so bashful. 'These women were actors of comedies, which pass there from island to island to play, as our players do here from town to town. . . . The greatest of their nobility travelling hold it no disgrace to send for these panders to their inn . . . either to fill their drink at table (for all men of any rank have their drink filled to them by women) or otherwise to have the use of them. When any of these panders die, though in their life time they were received into company of the best, yet now, as unworthy to rest amongst the worst, they are bridled with a bridle made of straw as you would bridle a horse and in the clothes they died in, are dragged through the streets into the fields, and there cast upon a dunghill, for dogs and fouls to devour.'

The day after this diversion Saris once again found himself faced with a disciplinary problem in the shape of 'one Christopher Evans', the gunner's mate, 'making a common practice of going ashore and lying out of the ship without leave, and in most lewd fashion spending his time in base bawdy places, denying to come aboard'. Saris had the offender clapped 'in the bilboes'. Given the character of Saris's recent visitors and his predilection for nude paintings this may have struck the condemned man as rather inconsistent behaviour on the part of his captain. His confinement, however, was lifted after two days, Saris and his fellow officers learning that he might break out of his prison anyway and use his knowledge of explosives to blow up the ship.

The next week passed without incident as the house ashore was made ready for occupation, though the English were amused to learn that their reputation had preceded them:

'our English nation hath been long known by report among

them, but much scandalled by the Portugals Jesuits as pirates and rovers upon the seas; so that the naturals [i.e. natives] have a song ... showing how the English do take the Spanish ships ... with which song and acting they terrify and scare their children.'

Troubles with the crew continued, 'one Jasper, a Fleming, one of our carpenters' being sent back to the ship for having 'abused the Captain China [i.e. Andrea Dittis] very grossly' and 'throwing his dishes about the house'. As nobody else had disliked the food and as Saris no doubt wished to placate his landlord 'who we find a great friend and willing to pleasure us in what he can', he commanded the boatswain's mates to 'bang the said Fleming with a rotan [rattan, i.e. cane], which they denied to do, being both drunk, wherefore, I banged them soundly and caused the master to beat the Fleming well.'

Saris was no doubt relieved when half the ship's company was able to move ashore on 1 July. With space to move about in and useful work to do in sorting out the cargo the members of his unruly crew might prove a little more tractable to discipline. In fact the day was to see the most dangerous incident to date, thanks to young Richard Wickham 'falling at words' with a Spanish member of the crew and challenging him to a duel. Richard Cocks, who was to become the head of the English factory, swiftly intervened to make the two men put up their weapons. The Spaniard obeyed at once but Wickham refused and stood his ground, swearing at Cocks in defiance. A crowd soon gathered but Saris was able to order the men back aboard. Upon investigation he decided that Wickham's quick temper was to blame and so sent the Spaniard back ashore and had Wickham's chest and bedding brought back aboard again 'purposing to let him rest till he better understand himself'. Saris then no doubt heaved a great sigh of relief, knowing full well that 'if they had drawn it might have brought both ourselves, ship and goods in danger for the custom here is that, whoever draws a weapon in anger, albeit he do no hurt therewith, is presently cut in pieces, and doing but a small hurt, not only themselves are executed, but their whole kindred.' Saris reasoned that 'if it be thus with them, it is not good for strangers having no privilege to presume over much'.

The day after this narrow escape Saris tried to make a price-fixing agreement with Brouwer. By the following morning, he found that the Dutchman had 'shipped away great store of cloth to divers islands, rating them at base prices ... that he might procure the more speedy dispatch of his own, and glut the place before the coming of ours'. Saris took what consolation he could in sending another letter to the still absent Adams. The next day he got Ho-in to prevent Brouwer from leaving for Edo, fearing that he intended to intercept and delay Adams. This favour cost Cocks his gold ring, which the daimyo admired — 'it was by counsel thought good to bestow it on him and Mr. Cocks to allow himself for it.'

When it turned out the next day that Brouwer, in defiance of the daimyo's orders, had stolen off to Nagasaki all Ho-in could do was seize the house and goods of the boatman who took him and imprison his family. Brouwer returned, however, within twenty-four hours, and informed Saris that a junk from Siam had docked in Nagasaki with a cargo of Brazil wood 'for the account of the English company'. Twenty-four hours later Brouwer sent 'a letter certifying me that he had mistaken himself and that sickness and overwaking was the occasion thereof. The truth being that no such wood as he formerly had told me was come for the account of the English'. Brouwer said that the wood instead belonged to the master of the junk, a Dutchman, a former shipmate of Adams aboard the *Liefde*. Suspecting that he had been swindled, Saris sent Cocks to Brouwer, 'to will him to consider better of the matter, for I would not be jested with, and that if he could not show me better proof of the bargain made than his own word, I would, as little knowledge as I had in the country, take that course as should not be pleasing to him'. Cocks returned with Brouwer's reply that he had now bought the wood from the junk-master and 'cared not what course I could take'. Saris, therefore, appealed to Ho-in to sequestrate the disputed goods and allow 'no sale made thereof till Mr. Addams came'. This was promptly done, the official responsible making 'a good jest of Mr. Brouwer's choler in this course'.

On 8 July the Englishman saw another and more terrible example of swift Japanese justice:

'three Japonians were executed, viz two men and one woman; the cause this: The woman, none of the honestest, her husband being travelled from home, had appointed these two their several hours to repair unto her. The latter man not knowing of the former, and thinking the time too long, coming in before the hour appointed, found the first man with her already, and enraged thereat, he whipped out his cattan [sword] and wounded both of them very sorely, having very nearly hewn the chine [length] of the man's back in two. But as well as he might he cleared himself of the woman and, recovering his cattan, wounded the other. The street taking notice of the fray, forthwith seized upon them, led them aside and acquainted King Foyne [Ho-in] ... who presently gave orders that they should cut off their heads: which done, every man that listed (as very many did) came to try the sharpness of their cattans upon the corpses, so that before they left off, they had hewn them all three into pieces as small as a man's hand, and yet notwithstanding did not then give over, but placing the pieces one upon another, would try how many of them they could strike through at a blow.'

This demonstration of Ho-in's absolute authority was followed by a rather strange reassurance of his continuing friendship. At dead of night Cocks and his interpreter were brought to the daimyo's residence, where he apologized 'that he came not so often to visit me as formerly' and explained that he believed he was under surveillance by one of Ieyasu's spies. As a token of his regard, however, he presented Saris with one of his favourite swords, a special mark of esteem. He also took the opportunity to advise the English not to set their prices too high, 'the Flemings ... having much hindered themselves in that way'. Ieyasu, he was sure, would buy most of what the English had to sell, and he and his friends would certainly be customers as well.

On the following day three more executions took place, this time as a punishment for abducting a woman.

On 11 July Saris was visited by 'Melser van Jonford' (Melchior van Santvoort), Adams's old shipmate, homeward bound from a trading voyage to Siam. Saris accepted some letters addressed to Adams and, finding the Dutchman much to his liking, offered him hospitality and a free trip back to England, 'but he refused both, being better affected to this course of life, holding it far more contenting than if he were in his own country'. He left the next day, having given Saris much valuable information about local trading conditions.

Another week passed in unloading and sorting the ship's cargo and the giving of more presents. On 20 July Saris was dismayed to have one of his letters to Adams returned to him undelivered. On the 21st the Dutch junk-master turned up with a letter for Adams and declared that he would prove the load of wood from Siam was rightfully his. Saris decided to let the matter rest until Adams made his much longed-for appearance. Ho-in meanwhile volunteered the information that the junk-master was 'of no account and very much indebted'.

On 25 July Saris determined to allow his men to break the monotony of waiting by celebrating the anniversary of King

James's coronation: 'I ordered eleven pieces ordnance to be shot off, our ship to put abroad all her gallantry, which the naturals took great notice of, the king much commending our order in remembering our duty. And in the afternoon visiting his majesty at his court, he bestowed upon me a fair armour, which he said he would give at this present for that he held it of some esteem, having worn it in the wars of Corea [i.e. Korea] ... I embraced his love and received his present with nine pieces ordnance in honour thereof, which gave him such great content that he began a health of a pint of admirable strong wine to his Majesty of England, causing his secretary to go forth and see that all that came with me had the same.'

Saris returned Ho-in's hospitality the following day, 'the old king ... entreating me to pardon his boldness, saying he held his time well passed in my company. And willed me to hold myself as welcome to Ferando as in my own country, and for that Mr. Addams stayed long, if I pleased he would fit me with a bark of speed to keep the shore between this and the Straits of Shemenaseque [i.e. Shimonoseki] to see if they could hear of him there, for the winds westerly was the occasion he came not. I accepted of his kindness and dispatched ... Mr. Addams host, thinking the time long till he came'.

Two days later Saris's Chinese landlord made a bet with him for ten pieces of eight that Adams would arrive within four days — 'which I accepted of, wishing to lose so he were come, or that there was no such in the country, for expecting him I do nothing but lie at charge'.

The next day Saris lost his bet.

10

'a naturalised Japanner'

'Giving so admirable and affectionated commendations of the country as it is generally thought amongst us that he is a naturalized Japanner.'
JOURNAL OF CAPTAIN JOHN SARIS

In his account of his first meeting with William Adams Saris takes great pains to stress the courtesies he extended to his exiled countryman and the eccentric manner in which they were received. A three-gun salute greeted Adams's arrival aboard the *Clove*. Then Saris 'sent Mr. Cocks and Mr. Peacock' in his 'skiff, fitted very comely for him' and gave the party a nine-gun salute on their landing ashore, 'where I received him in the best manner I could for his better grace'.

When Saris began to talk shop Adams's response, in marked contrast to that of van Santvoort, was surprisingly non-committal, saying that trade 'was not always alike, but sometimes better, sometimes worse'.

When they went into detail Adams was, according to his own subsequent account, far from encouraging about the prospects for the sale of the *Clove's* particular cargo: 'finding that such things as he had brought was not very vendible, I told him for his arrival I was very glad thereof, but in respect of the venture by the worshipful company being so great, I did not see any ways in this land to requite the great charges thereof. My reason was for their cloth at this present was very cheap, because both from Nova Spania, Manilia and out of Holland, which in these four years there came very much, some sold and very much unsold. For elephant teeth the Hollanders had brought abundance, that the price thereof was fallen very much, upon which occasion the Hollanders have transported many thereof to Siam. Steel in long bars still holding to its old price.... Lead holding its price a little more or less.... Tin so good cheap here as in England and ordnance not in any great request.... For calicoes ... not in any request, because this country hath abundance of cotton. Thus for those things. Now for pepper and cloves. This country doth ... not use much thereof, nor of any other spice.'

Saris then invited his guest to pick a room and order a meal of his choice. But Adams begged pardon of his would-be host and insisted on returning to his regular local lodgings — 'neither would he admit of any merchant or other to accompany him, which unto us all was very strange.' According to his own account Saris did what he could to disguise his annoyance. 'I would not further importune him till more acquaintance, praying him to do what he thought best, but withal to remember I was alone and should be glad to enjoy his most acceptable company, which I had long expected'. Adams promised to come when sent for and left abruptly after 'a short dinner', 'many proffering after he came down to go along in company with him in love, but he entreated the contrary, as some were not well pleased, thinking that he thought them not good enough to walk with him'.

The following day was eventful enough for any taste. In the morning a man was 'cut to pieces in the street' on a charge of incest with his mother; and his servant, on seeking to defend him, suffered a like fate. Adams again visited the *Clove* but 'made a little stay' apparently preferring the companionship of 'divers Spaniards and Portugales' whom Saris believed to be deserters from Vizcaino's expedition, sheltered by Adams from pursuit. When they begged to take passage with him to Bantam, Saris refused, feeling, no doubt, that he had an unreliable enough crew already. And that evening, as if to prove his judgement, Christopher Evans, having solemnly sworn not to go ashore again without leave, did so.

Two days after Adams's arrival Saris, having discussed the matter with his fellow merchants, decided to give him various presents (mostly clothes and textiles) 'whereby he might have some feeling of his brothers', thus taking the worldly-wise view 'no penny, no paternoster in this age'. Saris's own gifts to Adams were valued at more than twice what was given from the common store for such purposes and the total amounted to almost as much as they were to give to Hidetada himself. Adams reciprocated with a couple of token gifts of such insignificance that Saris, who 'kindly accepted' them, must have been as much mystified as insulted by the gesture.

When Adams visited the Dutchman Brouwer's house the following day, Saris persuaded him to take Cocks along 'willing him to take notice of the Fleming's usage of him, which was but ordinary'. Indeed, Cocks thought that the way in which the Dutch required

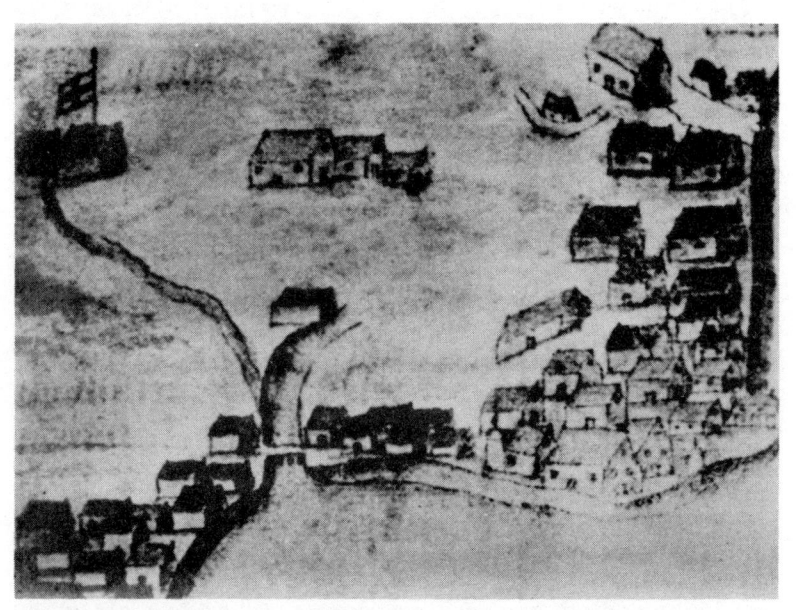

Picture of the English house at Hirado about 1621. St George's Cross is seen flying over the house in the top left-hand corner.

the pilot to account for certain goods he was handling on their behalf showed him scant respect indeed.

On 3 August 'by much entreaty' Adams was at last persuaded to stay with the English overnight and to give detailed advice regarding the presents that should be given to Ieyasu, Hidetada and the chief court officials. The next day, however, Adams spent in entertaining Spanish and Portuguese friends from Nagasaki and showing them over the *Clove*. Saris accepted the situation with good grace and 'sent order aboard to see he were well used and his friends'.

On 5 August the English party was at last ready to leave for the court. But Ho-in came in person to delay their departure because the retainer he wished to send with them was not yet ready. Adams, who, according to Saris, was not well-disposed towards the man in question, objected but was overruled, whereupon he went out to dinner again with his Spanish friends, despite Saris's entreaties for his continued company, advice and services as an interpreter.

The next day Saris delivered to Cocks and the master of the *Clove* detailed written instructions regarding the conduct of affairs in his absence. Cocks was warned not to sell any of the munitions, lead, tin or fine textiles because Adams believed that Ieyasu would buy all there was. Pepper, ivory and cloves, however, he could sell at his discretion. As for the English broadcloth, which was one of their most plentiful commodities, this too was to be set aside for Ieyasu on the somewhat paradoxical grounds that it was 'so evil-conditioned, coarse and high-priced, there is otherwise little hope that it will be vented' [i.e. sold]. James Foster, the master, was likewise warned to keep a close eye on various known trouble-makers, to control the crew's drinking as well as he might and to check the steward's accounts of the weekly consumption of provisions. On the other hand he was advised that if Ho-in or his grandson should decide to come aboard 'make no spare at such a time'. Finally, with regard to the Dutch, he was required to requite kindness with kindness and the least discourtesy with unmistakable reproof.

Troubles with the crew seem to have continued until the very moment of Saris's departure. Evans, having stolen ashore yet again to spend the night in female company had to be hauled back by main force. Unrepentant, Evans, being 'examined concerning the course of his disorder, stood boldly in that he was a man and would have a woman if he could get her'. At the same time evidence also came to light of Evans's intention to desert and take others with him. Anxious to get away, Saris left orders for his confinement below decks once more, and instructions that he should be released upon 'any hope of amendment'. Fransisco, earlier the thief of 'John Japan's cloak', having now stolen a sack of pepper from a shipmate's cabin, was treated with similar lenience and forgiven on grounds of youth and repentance.

Renouncing the part of Solomon, Saris rowed ashore with Cocks who informed him en route that the first mate 'was a private stirrer of the company to mutiny for fresh victual, saying it was not fit men should be fed in harbour with salt meat, yet to my face seemeth most officious. God deliver me from such dissembling false-tongued people'. Saris accordingly 'sent word to the master that he should have a care to let the company have what victuals in his discretion he did think fit'. And then, at last, at the head of his party of eighteen, Saris set forth, preceded by 'one Japanner, to carry my pike, accordingly to the custom of the country'.

11
'the King of England's letter'

'The 8 September I delivered the emperor the King of England's letter and his present, also a present from myself of my own goods, being, as Mr. Adams said, the fashion of the country.'
JOURNAL OF CAPTAIN JOHN SARIS

Saris's attempt to follow 'the fashion of the country' did not protect his party from unwelcome attention: 'at our landing and ... through the whole country, whithersoever we came, the boys, children and worser sort of idle people, would gather about and follow along after us.' Name-calling was usual, and sometimes, but rarely, accompanied by stone-throwing.

Like the 'Governor of Manilia' Saris found each successive city more impressive than the last. Hakata was 'as great as London is within the walls', Osaka had 'a castle in it, marvellous large and strong' and Suruga proved to be 'full as big as London, with all the suburb'.

Nor did the journey fail to provide a series of remarkable sights. Soon after leaving Hirado they came across 'women divers, that lived with their household and family upon the water, as in Holland they do the like'. As a result of regularly diving 'eight fathom deep' 'their eyes ... do grow as red as blood'. Next they saw 'a junk of 800 or 1,000 tons of burden, sheathed all with iron ... built in a very homely fashion, much like that which describeth Noah's Ark unto us. The naturals told us that she served to transport soldiers into any of the islands, if rebellion or war should happen.' Passing by the castle at Fushimi the party witnessed a change-over of garrisons. The English were greatly impressed by the splendour and dignity of the troops and not least by their discipline and the organization which saw to their provisioning: 'no man either travelling or inhabiting upon the way where they lodged but cheerfully entertained them as other their guests, because they paid for what they took, as other men did'.

They also had time to notice the ordinary and everyday aspects of Japanese life. With regard to food, Saris noted that one sort of rice was valued more than another, and that fish, pickles and game were important elements of customary fare. His observations were, however, sometimes faulty. Correctly recording that 'Butter they make none, neither will they eat any milk, because they hold it to be as blood', he nevertheless asserts that 'of cheese they have plenty'. But this is surely a confusion with *tofu* [bean-curd], which, at first glance, might be mistaken for it. The roads themselves were also worthy of note being 'divided into leagues [probably the Japanese *ri* of 2.45 miles] and at every leagues' end are two small hills, of either side of the way one, and upon every one of them a fair pine tree. ... These marks are placed upon the way to the end, that the hackney men and those which let out horses to hire, should not make men pay more than their due.' There were also the grim reminders of Japanese justice, 'divers crosses with the dead corpses of these which had been executed remaining still upon them, and the pieces of others, which after their executions had been hewn again and again by trial of others' cattans. All which caused a most unsavoury passage to us.'

Arriving at Suruga, after nearly a month on the road, the party 'being somewhat weary' rested for a day before presenting themselves at Ieyasu's palace with King James's letter and gifts of the East India Company. According to Adams they were 'courteously received and bid welcome by the treasurer and others' but Saris immediately soured the atmosphere by trying to cut across the conventions of court etiquette. Adams found himself caught in the cross-fire:

'the general [i.e. Saris] called me and bid me tell the secretary that the king's majesty's letter he would deliver it with his own hands. Upon which I went and told the secretary thereof: at which he answered that it was not the custom of the land to deliver any letter with the hand of any stranger, but that he should keep the letter in his hand till he came into the presence of the emperor, and then he would take it from him out of his hands and deliver it to the emperor. Which answer I told the general thereof, at which answer not being contented caused me to tell the secretary that if he might not deliver it himself he would return again to his lodging. Which second answer I told the secretary, the which answer, not thinking well thereof, was discounted with me in that I had not instructed him in the manners and custom of all strangers which had been yearly in their country; and made me again to go to the general, the which I did, but the general being very much discontented, it so rested.'

Saris and Adams, in their respective accounts of the audience with Ieyasu, differ considerably in the significance each assigns to the other, and contradict each other flatly in the contentious matter of the letter. Adams records Ieyasu 'receiving his majesty's letter from the general by the hands of the secretary'. Saris however stresses the closeness of his contact with the former shogun:

'Coming to the emperor, according to our English compliments, I delivered our king's letter unto his majesty, who took it in his hand and put it up towards his forehead, and commanded his interpreter, who sat a good distance from him behind, to will Master Adams to tell me that I was welcome from a wearisome journey, that I should take my rest for a day or two, and then his answer should be ready for our king.'

Saris then withdrew, Ieyasu having offered him men and horses to enable him to visit Hidetada at Edo. Saris makes no mention of the fact that Adams did not leave with him and that, indeed, a lengthy interview then took place between Ieyasu and the pilot. According to Adams, 'the general departed his way, and I was called in, to whom the emperor inquired of me of the king's majesty of England, concerning his greatness and power, with divers other questions which were too long to write. Only at the last he bid me tell the general that what request he had, that he should make it known to me, or to go to his secretary, he should be answered; which answer to the general.'

The next day Adams and Saris went to the secretary's house. Saris records that the official returned the gift offered to him at that time 'saying it were as much as his life were worth if he should take anything, the emperor having forbidden him'. He also advised them to state their requests as concisely as possible 'for the people of Japan affect brevity'.

On 10 September Adams delivered the abbreviated articles and found himself once again the subject of searching enquiries from Ieyasu. The question of trading privileges did not, however, form the main subject of their conversation: 'the emperor read all his demands, and having read them told me that he should have them.' He subsequently revoked, after protests from the Chinese ambassador, the right to seize Chinese ships and goods, China having refused to trade with England. Ieyasu was much more concerned to find out whether the English had any other motives in coming to his domains and other long-term objectives to pursue:

'having had much speech here and there, he asked me if part of his [i.e. Saris's] coming was not for to discover farther parts to the northwestward or northwards. I told him our country still doth not cease to spend much money in discovery thereof. He asked me whether there were not a way and whether it was not very short or near. I told him we doubted not but there is a way and that very near, at which time called for a map of the whole world, and so saw that it was very near. Having speeches with me, whether we had no knowledge of a land lying hard by his country, on the north part of his land, called Yedzoo [i.e. Hokkaido]. I told him I did never see it put into any map or globe. I told him it might be that the worshipful company would send some ship, or other, to discover.... He asked if I did desire to go that way. I told him, if the worshipful company should desire such a thing, I would willingly employ myself in such an honourable action. He told me if I did so, he would give me his letter of friendship to the land of Yedzoo, where his subjects have friendship, having a strong town and a castle ... and so thus, with divers other speeches most friendly used, I took my leave of him.'

12

'to go for my country'

'He looked earnestly upon me, and asked me if I was desirous to go for my country? I answered most desirous.'
LETTER OF WILLIAM ADAMS, DECEMBER 1613

On 12 September Saris, Adams and their attendants left for Edo, evidently in holiday mood, for coming upon the town of Kamakura's gigantic statue of a Buddha they treated it with touristic disrespect, notwithstanding the fact that the image was 'much reverenced by travellers as they pass there'. Saris later admitted that 'Some of our people went into the body of it and ... made an exceeding great noise. We found many characters and marks made upon it by passengers, whom some of my followers imitated and made theirs in like manner.'

Edo, when they reached it after two days on the road, 'made a very glorious appearance unto us; the ridge tiles and corner-tiles richly gilded, the posts of their doors gilded and varnished; glass windows they have none, but great windows of board, opening in leaves, well set out with painting, as in Holland. There is a causeway which goes through the chief street of the town; underneath this causeway runs a river; at every fifty paces there is a well-head, fitted very substantially of free-stone, with buckets for the neighbours to fetch water, and for danger of fire. This street is as broad as any of our streets in England.'

Like Don Rodrigo before him, Saris observed that Hidetada's fortress was much stronger than Ieyasu's but his interview with the shogun passed off less eventfully than his predecessor's and he departed bearing two swords for himself and two suits of armour for King James.

The following few days were spent at Adams's estate to the south, overlooking Uraga Bay. Saris's favourable appreciation of the commercial potential of the location is very significant in view of the later decision to site the English trading-post at Hirado. It was, he recorded, 'a very good harbour for shipping where ships may ride as safely as in the river of Thames before London, and the passage thereto by sea very safe and good; so that it will be much better for our ships to sail thither than to Firando [Hirado], in respect that Oringgaw [Uraga] is upon the main island, and is distant from Edo but fourteen or fifteen leagues. The place is not so well replenished with victual and fleshmeat as Firando is, which want only excepted, Oringgaw is for all other matters to be preferred before Firando'.

During his stay Saris 'bargained with Mr. Addams for the hull of a ship which was the Spaniards'.... The ship he asked £100 for and would abate nothing thereof, which to our judgements was very dear.' Saris did, however, 'also look upon certain wares of Meaco [Myako, i.e. Kyoto] which he had there of the Spaniards' to sell' and bought a number of items of furniture. Hard bargaining did not, however, seem to damage the relationship between host and guests and presents of cloth and a silver-gilt cup were given to 'Mistris Addams', her sister and mother 'in regard to her husband's kindness'.

Returning to Ieyasu's court at Suruga Saris had occasion to witness a dramatic instance of diplomatic failure:

'At my return... I found a Spanish ambassador arrived there from the Philippines, who only had sight of the emperor, and delivered him his presents.... After the first time, he could not obtain access to the emperor. His embassy was that such Portuguese and Spaniards as were within his dominions, not authorized by the King of Spain, might be delivered up unto him to carry away... which the emperor denied to do saying that his country was a free country and none should be forced out of it, but if the ambassador could persuade any to go, they should not be stayed. This coming of the Spanish ambassador for men was caused by the great want of men they had to defend the Molucca islands from the Dutch, who then made great preparation for the absolute conquest thereof. After that the ambassador had attended for the emperor's answer the time limited him by his commission, seeing it come not, he departed discontented.'

After ten days Saris, by contrast, received from Ieyasu a written confirmation of the right of English traders:

— to enter and leave Japan freely and stay or leave at their pleasure;

— to pay no tariffs and pay no special suit to the court whenever they traded;

— to call upon Japanese help in the event of storm and shipwreck;

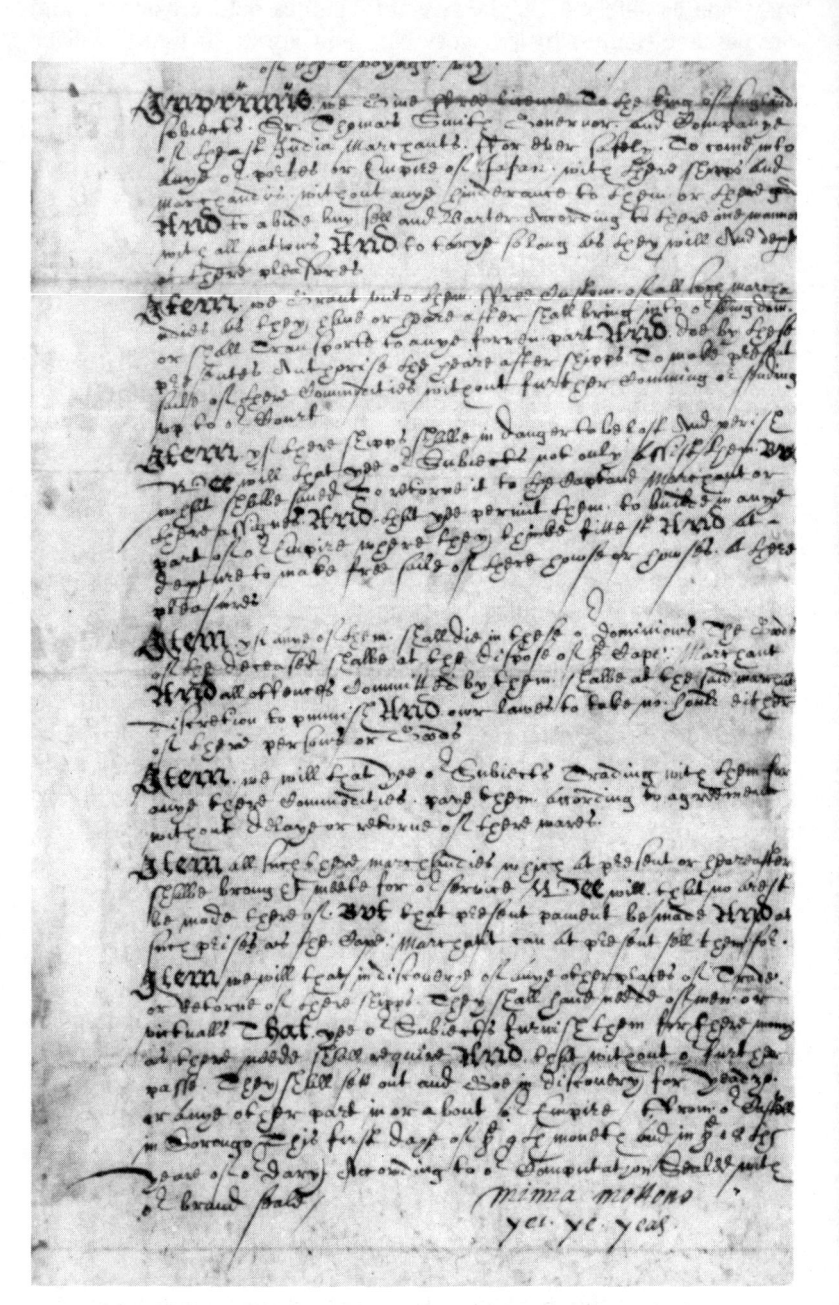

A copy of the privileges granted to the East India Company by Tokugawa Ieyasu.

— to build and dispose of houses and buildings ashore;
— to be tried by their own laws in the event of committing a crime;
— to receive prompt payment upon conclusion of a bargain.

This grant was accompanied by a most handsomely worded letter:

'Your Majesty's kind letter sent me by your servant, Captain John Saris, which is the first that I have known to arrive in any part of my dominions, I heartily embrace, being not a little glad to hear of your great wisdom and power, having three mighty and plentiful kingdoms under your worthy command, acknowledging your majesty's great bounty in sending many rare things such as my land affordeth not, neither have I before time seen. The which I receive, not as from a stranger but as from your majesty, whom I esteem as myself, desiring the continuance of friendship with your highness. And that it may stand with your good liking to send your subjects to any port or part of my dominions, where they shall be most heartily welcome, applauding much their worthiness in the admirable knowledge of navigation, having with much facility discovered so remote a place, being no whit amazed with the distance of so mighty a gulf, nor greatness of such infinite clouds and storms, from prosecuting honourable enterprises of discovery and merchandising, in which they shall find me to further them according to their desires.

'I return your majesty a small token of my love by your said subject, desiring you to accept thereof, as from him which rejoiceth much in your friendship.

'And whereas your majesty's subjects have desired certain privileges for trade and settling of a factory in my dominions I have not only granted to what they demanded, but have given it under my broad [great] seal, for the better performance thereof.

'From my castle in Suruga this 4th day of the 9th month and in the 18th year of our emperor according to our computation. Resting your majesty's friend, highest commander in this kingdom of Japan.

Minamoto no Ieyasu'

Encouraged by this success, Adams in his own words, 'made my self somewhat bold' and approached the emperor on a matter long close to his heart. 'Finding the emperor in a good mood, I took out of my bosom his broad seal, concerning certain lands [i.e. Adams's estate] and laid it down befre him, giving his majesty most humble thanks for his great favour unto me, desiring leave to go for my country. At which request he looked earnestly upon me and asked me if I was desirous to go for my country? I answered most desirous. He answered, if he should detain me, he should do me wrong; in so much, that in his service I had behaved myself well, with many other words of commendations. . . . So I thank God got my liberty.'

'Being not little joyful' Adams joined Saris on his way back to Hirado. The route took them via Kyoto, which took them a week to reach, owing to heavy rains. Here they received a present of ten painted screens from the emperor, whom, like other foreigners, they never actually saw. But like Don Rodrigo before them, they found time to visit both Hideyoshi's tomb and the Great Buddha at Nara. Just over a fortnight later they arrived back at Hirado.

13

'in the General's absence'

'I verily think the old king took notice of some of our men's evil behaviour this last night. For he willed me . . . that matters, might be as well managed in the General's absence as when he was here present; otherwise the shame would be ours but the dishonour his.'
DIARY OF RICHARD COCKS, 7 AUGUST 1613

The parting instructions left by Saris show that he anticipated trouble in his absence. He was not alone in this, for the day after he departed Cocks went to thank the daimyo, Ho-in, for his assistance in providing men and horses for the journey and, having been complimented on his courtesy, was warned that the untoward behaviour of the crew had not passed unnoticed and that a firm hand should be kept on them.

On the following day a Spanish-speaking Japanese-Christian boy called Juan came to Cocks and asked to be taken into his service, to enable him to travel to England. Cocks bought him some new clothes and took him on, being dissatisfied with Miguel, the interpreter left behind by Adams, because he was 'something stubborn and loved to run abroad at his pleasure, leaving me without anyone that could speak a word'.

Almost a fortnight after the departure of Saris and his party there took place the summer festival of O-bon, when the graves of the dead were cleaned in remembrance and candles and fires are lit to guide their spirits to a symbolic reunion with the living. Ho-in's instructions to spread fresh gravel and to light lanterns before one's house were followed with alacrity by the English party, Cocks having learned that 'a poor man was put to death and his house shut up for disobeying therein'. He also prudently sent presents 'of wine and banqueting stuff' to the daimyo, his relatives and officials.

The three-day festival having ended, the energies of the crew were bent to the seemingly endless task of unloading cargo. In a sense it was a task they had brought upon themselves because they had begun 'to filch and steal to go to taverns and whore-houses'.

At the end of the first week in September Cocks and his

companions endured their first typhoon. It was preceded by 'much rain, with wind increasing all day and night variable', and according to Cocks the storm 'overthrew one hundred houses in Firando and uncovered many others', as well as whipping up the sea to undermine the Dutch factory's stone wharf and sink forty or fifty boats at anchor. The 'English house' suffered the loss of a newly built kitchen wall 'and did shake like as if there had been an earthquake'. One can well believe that Cocks 'never passed night in all my life in such fear', not least because 'barbarous unruly people did run up and down the streets all night with fire-brands ... so that the greatest fear I had was that all would have been consumed with fire'. The *Clove* meanwhile 'rode at anchor with five cables, and as many anchors, whereof one old cable burst, but God be thanked no other hurt done'.

Five days later, after some inconclusive bargaining with a couple of Kyoto traders, Cocks found himself having to cope with the well-established problem of discipline:

'Francis Williams, being drunk ashore, did strike one of the old king's men with a cudgel, which gave him no occasion at all, nor spake a word to him. The man came to the English house and complained, being very angry (and not without cause) giving me to understand that he would inform the king his master how he was misused by our people. He had three or four in company with him, who did see him abused and that he which did it was newly gone aboard the ship.' Cocks, therefore, 'gave them fair words and desired them to go aboard and find out the party and they should see him punished to their contents'. This they did, but when they saw Williams, still evidently very drunk, dragged to the capstan for chastisement, they 'entreated for his pardon'.

Any effect this episode might have had on the rest of the crew soon evaporated. Two days later the master informed Cocks that 'most part of the ship's company had lain ashore all night without asking him leave, notwithstanding the great wind which had continued all night, and the ship on ground'. They were found drinking, gambling and quarrelling over women. Some were cuffed into obedience but several, two of whom 'went into a field and fought', remained obdurate. Three days afterwards the master of the brothel boldly announced that any ship's officer who tried to take back a member of his crew by force would be killed. Cocks went straight to Ho-in, who issued a proclamation forbidding any Japanese to keep foreigners within his house after sundown and empowering Cocks to seek out his men without hindrance. The

Scene from the pleasure quarters of the Yoshiwar district painted by Hisikawa Moronubu (d.1694).

effect of this announcement appears to have been counter-productive because 'this angered our people in such sort that some of them gave it out they would drink in the fields, if they might not be suffered to do it in the town, for drink they would, although they sought it in the country.'

Ten days later the first mate died after a protracted illness. Ho-in gave permission for a Christian burial but the protests of local Buddhist priests obliged the foreigners to take the corpse to its resting-place by a roundabout route on a boat rather than through the streets of the town. And even then they had 'much ado' to find a grave-digger.

On 2 October the master of the *Clove* sent word to Cocks that half a dozen of the crew, including, predictably enough, Christopher Evans, had deserted in the ship's skiff. Cocks, hearing that they were 'making merry at a tap-house' hurried to track them down, only to find that 'they proved to be others' — 'so in the mean time our runaways had the more time to run away'. Ho-in, in this case, could render no immediate assistance, for that same night his palace had burned down. When, however, Cocks received word that the deserters were on a certain 'desert island' Ho-in promised to do all in his power to bring them back 'either alive or dead; yet they would be loathe to kill them, in respect we might want men to carry our ship back for England. I gave them thanks for the care they had of us; yet withal gave them to understand that although these knaves miscarried, we had honest men enough to sail the ship for England.' The daimyo thereupon 'made ready two boats full of soldiers to go after them, with full determination to bring them back either alive or dead'. Two days later he sent out another two boat-loads of soldiers. But by that time the fugitives had hidden themselves in the back streets of Nagasaki and Cocks was brought to understand that Miguel, the interpreter supplied by Adams, had in fact helped them cover their tracks. Cocks therefore, appealed to the governor of Nagasaki, who agreed to return the deserters after Cocks, with some reluctance, agreed not to punish them. He then continued the soft-soap treatment by banqueting the Japanese aboard the *Clove* and gratifying such whims as for a quantity of large cloves, a monkey and a telescope.

A fortnight after the deserters left, Cocks learned from a Dutchman and an Italian, who claimed to be well known to William Adams, that they had sailed off in an open boat for Macao.

Three days later a fire raged through the town by night destroying forty houses. This disaster gave Cocks and his men an unexpected chance to shine, for 'had not our English men bestirred themselves lustily, many more houses had gone to wrack' with the result that they 'were very much commended of the kings and all other in general'. Even the Dutch offered to help the English carry away their goods to safety, should they be in danger of burning.

Further news from Nagasaki convinced Cocks that the runaways from his crew were beyond his reach. Ho-in could only promise to prevent further desertions by forbidding Japanese boatmen to 'carry or convey away any of our people, without making it known'.

Numerous minor incidents marked the passage of the following days: a 'great pagan festival' was celebrated by a mounted archery contest in the street, the Chinese landlord fell ill and begged from his sick bed for a piece of pork, would-be robbers tried to fire a number of houses in the town, the purser fell sick and tried Japanese medication to no effect and the local notables borrowed some English costumes for the performance of a 'comedy or play'. This last was evidently a very special occasion, 'the actors being kings themselves, with the greatest noblemen and princes. The matter was of the valiant deeds of their ancestors, from the beginning of their kingdom or commonwealth, until this present, with much mirth mixed among, to give the common people content. The audience was great, for no house in town but brought a present, nor no village nor place under their dominions but did the like, and were spectators. And the kings themselves did see that every one, both great and small, did eat and drink before they departed'. Cocks did, however, feel obligated to record that 'their acting, music and singing, as also their poetry, is very harsh to us, yet they keep due time with both hands and feet.' On the other hand he was vastly impressed by the fact that he 'never saw play wherein I noted so much, for I see their policy is great in doing thereof, and quite contrary to our comedies in Christendom, ours but being dumb-shows, and thus the truth itself, acted by the kings themselves, to keep in perpetual remembrance their affairs'. Nor could he forebear to add that 'the king did not send for the Flemings and, therefore, I accounted it a greater grace for us'.

Returning home Cocks found himself awaited by 'three or four Flemings' who seemed to be engaged in illicit trade with Korea, apparently at Adams's instigation. Cocks's reaction was to hope that 'if they do well we cannot do amiss, M. Adams ... no doubt will be as forward for the good of his own country as for strangers'.

Later that evening two Spaniards turned up, claiming to bring news of the fugitives who were, they alleged, by no means the dupes of the Jesuits but rather of the wicked people of Nagasaki. Cocks, suspecting that they had in fact come to lure away more members of the crew, sent word to the master of the *Clove* 'to have a care both to ships and boats . . . for that it is good to doubt the worst, for the best will save itself'.

In fact, the following days brought nothing more alarming than a number of fire scares, an attempted robbery on a nearby house and a less than welcome visit from a Spanish Jesuit who was nevertheless kindly entertained: 'For as the old saying is, it is good sometimes to hold a candle to the devil.' No doubt Cocks was much relieved to welcome Saris and Adams on the following day.

14

'a profitable servant'

'God grant his blessings upon my labours, that I may be a profitable servant unto your worship, which I hope in almighty God I shall be.'
LETTER OF WILLIAM ADAMS, DECEMBER 1613

The day after his return Saris spent in visiting Ho-in to thank him for all that he had done in his absence. Adams was at the same time dispatched to Nagasaki to seek out the runaways. Having left his crew quarrelsome and criminous, Saris came back to find them in the same state, two men going secretly ashore to fight three nights after his return, with the result that the one was in danger of his life, and the other a lame man for ever, 'and that which was more, the survivor in danger to be hanged if the other died'. Ho-in, for all his friendliness towards the foreigners and his gratitude for their many gifts and entertainments, was furious and told Saris that 'if any more came ashore to fight and shed blood in his country (contrary to his laws) he would cause them to be cut to pieces, for that he would not suffer strangers to have more privilege in that matter than his own subjects'. This severe warning did not, however, prevent the daimyo from hinting that a few more gifts, to replace the ones destroyed when his home burned down, would not be unwelcome.

Word then came, in the person of a Spaniard from Nagasaki, that the runaways had indeed left the country altogether and, moreover, entirely on their own initiative, the Franciscans and Jesuits denying any hand in the matter — 'neither ever spoke such a word that we were heretics or thieves'. The messenger brought with him as gifts 'three baskets of sugar and a pot of conserves' but Saris was by no means inclined to accept his 'sugared, conserved words of compliment' and remained determined to 'hold these but words to excuse themselves and put other men in fault, for the Spaniards love not the Portugals, neither of both the Japan, much less the Japan them'.

Three days after this incident Adams returned from Nagasaki, confirming that the fugitives had taken ships for Macao and the Philippines. On the same day two officials came aboard the *Clove* to lay down the law to the crew: 'they which went out to fight and drew weapon were to die the death, and all those which did behold them [were] obliged to kill both parties in pain of ruinating all their generation.'

Two days later Saris proved to his own satisfaction that Adams's servant Miguel, who had been left to look after the English as interpreter and general go-between, had cheated them when buying drink on their behalf. 'In friendly manner I acquainted Mr. Adams, in the presence of Mr. Cocks of his man's dishonest and villainous dealing.... He took it very evil... and so highly took his part as by the persuasion of Mr. Cocks I did not say further but gave order to Mr. Cocks to let him go no more to market for us.'

The mood of the company was doubtless lightened a couple of days later when Ho-in visited them with a troupe of dancing bears, three whores and some travelling musicians. But the atmosphere of ill-feeling which had existed between Saris and Adams since the day of their first meeting could not be dispelled so easily and the imminent departure of the *Clove* brought matters to a head. Adams's account of the crucial interview which took place between them is both terse and illuminating. Saris wished 'to know of me what my intent was, whether I would go home with him, or tarry here in this country. I answered him my desire was to go home to my country. He asked me, now with him or no; I answered him, I had spent in this country many years, through which I was poor; for which case I was desirous to get something before my return.' (A curious excuse for a man with a country estate, a town house and a well-established trading agency.) In his account of his decision not to accept Saris's offer of a return passage to England, Adams does then admit that 'the reason I would not go with him was for divers injuries done against me; the which were things to me very strange and unlooked for'.

Adams having decided to stay on in Japan, Saris then negotiated with him the terms under which he might be employed as an agent by the East India Company. His first offer was that Adams would accept £20 which the Company had advanced to his wife in England as an outright grant and trust that a fair salary would be arranged in due course. Adams, while acknowledging 'this deed of Christian charity in the lending of my poor wife the £20', answered that if he were in England he might well have been willing to accept such terms 'but in this place, was willing to have some certainty'. Saris then asked him what sort of salary he looked for per year. Adams replied that he was used to hiring his services by the month rather than the year. Saris emphasized that it was Company policy to hire by the year and not the month. Adams rejoined that 'I was not willing to go by the year, but by the month'. Saris at length conceded the point and asked Adams how much he would expect to receive per month for his services. Adams told him that he usually got £15 a month from strangers, but that he would be willing to take £12. Saris then asked Adams to leave the room while he consulted his colleagues.

When Adams returned he offered him an annual salary of £80. Adams replied that he would accept nothing less than £10 a month and that as the Company might be hard put to find such a sum out of its likely profits from the Japan trade, he might as well trade on his own account and take full advantage of the privileged position he held in the country — 'desiring the general to let me be free, and to take other orders, which were for my furtherance and not to be here employed, where I saw no profit come in'. Saris again offered £80, plus the £20 already advanced to Adams's English wife. Adams refused but promised to come back the next day, when matters were finally resolved:

Saris 'the next day, in the morning, sent for me again [asking] whether I was resolved. I said as afore. So he answered me, I did exact upon them to have them to give me that I list. I told him again my meaning was not so, for I could better myself a great deal more.... So demanding me still earnestly [Saris] proffered me £100 the year, the which, in consideration I would not give discontentment, but granted unto it.' Adams's acceptance was, however, conditional upon being paid an advance on the agreed sum to maintain himself 'in credit and clothes'. (In fact this was no bad bargain, Cocks himself, as chief merchant, only received £150 and the others a mere £40.)

A few days after the conclusion of these proceedings word came that Palmer, one of the crewmen involved in the fracas which had occurred immediately after Saris's return, had at last died, in the opinion of the ship's surgeon, having been 'the occasion of his own death, his wound being curable, if he would have been ruled'. Saris gave orders for a secret burial on an offshore island, fearing that the Japanese he hoped to hire as auxiliary crewmen might be scared off if they knew of such events.

As the date of the *Clove*'s departure drew near, local Japanese

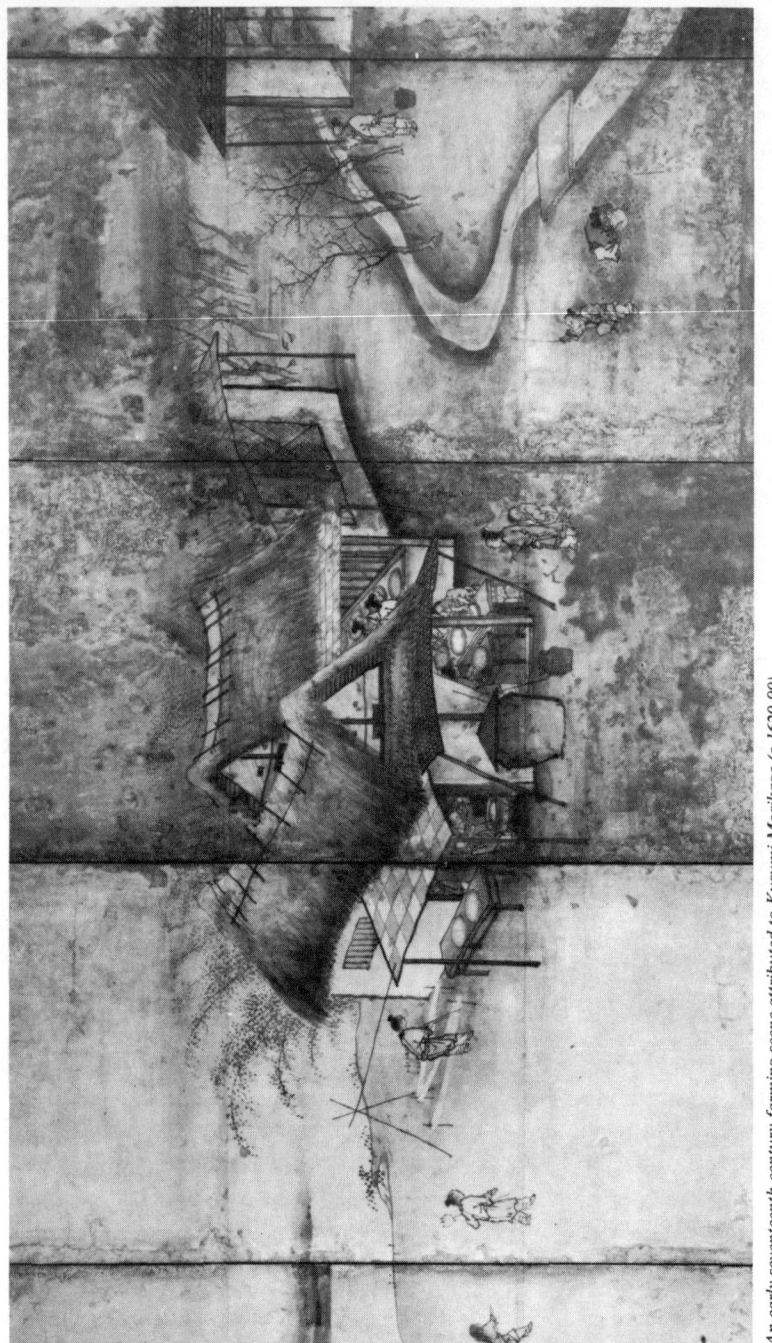

An early seventeenth century farming scene attributed to Kusumi Morikage (c.1620-90).

traders began to press for the repayment of credit extended to members of its crew. Saris ordered that appropriate sums should be stopped out of the men's wages. At the same time he also decided to site the English 'factory' at Hirado, where they could keep an eye on the Dutch, their main opposition. It was, therefore, determined that Cocks should be left in charge, along with seven other English employees of the company, three Japanese interpreters and two Japanese servants.

On 5 December Saris left Japan after a sojourn of six months, all but one week. He left behind, in a 'Remembrance' to Cocks, a singularly adverse opinion of the pilot whose political influence and diplomatic skill had won the company such extraordinary privileges: 'And for Mr. Adams, he is only fitting to be master of the junk and to be used as linguist at court, when you have no employment for him at sea. It is necessary you stir him... otherwise you shall have little service of him, the country affording great liberty, whereunto he is much affected.'

The document then claimed that Saris was more or less forced to offer Adams the terms he finally accepted by false offers of alternative employment by his Dutch and Spanish friends and the fact that the English simply had to secure his services being 'wholly destitute of language'. Saris finally warned Cocks that Adams was bound to pretend that it would be essential for him to have written permission from the shogun before he could take a ship out of Japanese waters but in fact this would be a mere ploy to enable Adams to claim the expenses for a trip to the capital and make a visit to his wife and estate at the same time. But Saris did not, for all his dislike, underestimate the value of Adams's services, and concluded with the advice that 'rather than that he should leave you, and betake himself to the Spaniards or Flemings, you must make a virtue of necessity and let him go [to Edo]'.

Subsequent events appear to have proved Saris mistaken or unjust — or both.

Adams did not show himself willing to put the interest of the Dutch or Spanish before those of the English. Neither did he go up to court to seek special permission before setting out to sea on behalf of his new employers. In the absence of more conclusive evidence the verdict on Saris's allegations must be at worst one of 'not proven'. In the event it was Saris whose good name was to suffer. On his return to England he was subjected to a lengthy enquiry at the hands of the East India Company regarding his conduct of the voyage. Found guilty of trading on his own account, a misdemeanour expressly forbidden by his instructions, he was dismissed from the service of the Company. Even more shamefully the man who kept a 'lascivious' painting of Venus in his cabin was found when it was further searched to have brought back an extensive collection of pornographic books and pictures. Scandalized, the directors of the East India Company ordered the offending articles to be publicly burned. The unruffled Saris retired to Fulham, married a grand-daughter of a Lord Mayor of London and died nearly thirty years later, a rich old man, noted for his pious benefactions to the poor.

After Saris's departure in the *Clove*, Cocks, as chief merchant, proceeded to establish a network of branches in the most populous parts of the country. Eaton was sent to Osaka and Wickham to Edo. Adams's father-in-law agreed to act as the company's agent in Kyoto and his brother-in-law served in the same capacity at Uraga. (Cocks later came to regard both these gentlemen as 'crafty knaves'.) Other Japanese were appointed at Nagasaki, Sakai (near Osaka) and Suruga. Adams's knowledge of the country and the language were naturally of very great value in carrying forward this ambitious enterprise but his new colleagues did not always take kindly to his advice. As early as January 1614 Cocks was writing to the quick-tempered Wickham in the following terms:

'I pray you have a good care to give Captain Adams content, which you may easily do if you use him with kind speeches and fall not into terms with him upon any argument. I am persuaded I could live with him seven years before any extraordinary speeches should happen betwixt us.'

Cocks's analysis of Adams's character was to prove more accurate than his prediction of their future relationship.

Wickham for his part, wrote to Cocks in May that 'I cannot tell what to think or speak of Captain Adams.... I much suspect playing of both sides.' He was also confused by the conflict between Adams's advice to follow normal Japanese custom and allow his customers to take away goods on credit and Cocks's strict instructions to insist on cash for every transaction. Wickham was also painfully conscious of his complete dependence on Adams in such important but tricky matters as local systems of weights and measures. When it was found, for instance, that a load of lead sold to Ieyasu as part of a consignment of munitions was short weight it was left entirely to Adams to sort the matter out.

In March 1614 Cocks sent two English merchants, Tempest Peacock and Walter Carwardine, to open up trade with Cochin-

China (Vietnam). In July Adams described their rumoured fate in a graphic letter to Wickham:

'we have had very bad news from Cochin-China of Mr. Peacock which, as we hear is killed with all the Hollanders that went in company.... As we hear the king bought all the goods of Mr. Peacock and the Hollanders... and a little before their being ready to depart... being embarked to return in a small boat the king sent a great boat... who followed the little boat and with force ran against the little boat and overthrew her that she did sink, and swimming in the water the Cochin-Chinas cut them all to pieces.'

Whether Carawardine was alive or dead or where he might be in either case no one yet knew.

Undeterred, Adams at Cocks's request, had, he told Wickham, bought a junk and begun fitting her out for a voyage to Siam. More was to be spent on repairing her than was laid out for her purchase in the first place. And much time and labour was to be expended by Adams in supervising the work. But on the eve of her departure, Cocks was able to write to the directors of the East India Company that Adams 'hath taken great pain about repairing our junk, the *Sea Adventure,* otherwise she would not have been ready to have made the Siam voyage this year.' Indeed, he concluded, 'I find the man very tractable and willing to do you Worships the best service he can.'

15

'a voyage to Siam'

'A voyage to Siam, which I pray God to prosper begun the 28 of November 1614 which day being Monday about 7 o'clock weighed my anchors.'
LOG BOOK OF WILLIAM ADAMS

Adams's first voyage to Siam never reached its destination or fulfilled its intended purpose. 'Contrary wind' prevented the *Sea Adventure* from leaving the coast of Kyushu until mid-December. Adams has left his own graphic account of the disastrous turn of events thereafter:

'two days after my departure ... a most grievous storm took me, called a hurricane, of violent wind, by which I was in great danger to lose both lives, ship and goods, for the space of three days bailing in four rooms [Japanese ships were built in separate watertight compartments], having with me at that time of officers, mariners and passengers forty souls; the which being wearied with a long storm, could not longer endure it; but the principal of them came to me and held up their hands, praying me to do my best to save their lives.... The thing which grieved me not a little [being not above twenty leagues from the coast of China] to go for China, being most bitter enemies to the Japanners, there we could not trim our ship, that I was fain to take another course, directed my course for certain islands called the Ryukyus, which through the blessing of God three days after arrived [at Oshima] in safety, to all our great rejoicing: for which God be praised for ever.'

Wickham, however, in a later letter to Cocks, attributed their deliverance to divine intervention, rather than the pilot's skill — 'the mercy of God exceeded our misery or else we had never seen land again' — and also recorded with irritation that 'the next day as we were weighing our anchor, the mariners through negligence let slip our best cable and anchor which there we left behind us'. By then, however, the crew, after a frantic search, had located one major leak and 'praying to God to find the rest' Adams had decided to make for a more suitable anchorage than Oshima in which to carry out the extensive repairs that were obviously going to be necessary.

Arriving safely at Okinawa and having received permission from the lord of the island to land his cargo, preparatory to undertaking the refitting of his ship, Adams found lodgings ashore 'where the goods and victuals were landed'. The crew were no doubt pleased to receive the rice, hams and vegetables sent by the lord as a gesture of goodwill. Unfortunately this early indication of co-operation did not accurately foreshadow the future course of events.

Having landed his cargo and selected a suitable place to beach the ship, Adams began to organize the crew into taking out the masts. But at this point the merchants aboard complained that the sailors, having no proper boatswain, ignored orders given to them direct. As pilot Adams had ultimate responsibility for the management of the crew and the safety of the ship and on this occasion managed to smooth things over: 'I desired them [i.e. the crew] as they had been true to me to this present that now in my need they would stand by me to help me, so we agreed.'

After another four days all the ballast had been cleared out but no further progress could be made because the local officials had failed to supply the timber and the other materials necessary to make a proper job of repairing the ship. Adams therefore called a meeting of all the officers and merchants to decide what course of action they should take, knowing full well that any lengthy delay would mean missing the monsoon winds which they needed to carry them to Siam. 'We concluded to trim our ship so well as we could and go forward in the voyage in the name of God.'

Having plugged a few minor holes, the company was then fortunate enough to be able to buy some timber and the lime and linseed necessary to make 'gallagall', a sort of water-resistant varnish. But when the lime turned out to be bad the English decided to go over the heads of the local officials and appeal to the lord direct for the materials they needed.

While awaiting a reply to this request Adams set his men to making ropes and two new cables to replace the one lost at Oshima. On 15 January court officials finally arrived, ordered the local authorities to supply the needed materials and invited Adams and his colleagues to a banquet. They returned the compliment with the inevitable presents.

Having made 'a warp [i.e. rope] of 130 fathoms for the river of

Siam' and mended various sails, the crew then set to work on caulking the ship, only to find, after a delay of a day spent celebrating the beginning of the new Japanese year, that their new load of lime was also useless. Adams thereupon set the men to making a new pump while a fresh load was burned for his use.

On 26 January, with the caulking, at last almost completed and the reloading of the ballast begun, Adams found himself faced with a strike — 'at noon our men would not come to work but would have their hire which was due to them in Siam, so I had much ado with them.' Negotiations continued the following day. 'I told them it was not due to them before they came to Siam at which place, God sending us thither, I would pay them and before I could not nor would not but if they had unright done them I would make them what satisfaction I should be appointed by the justice of Japan and thereupon to satisfy them I would give them a bill from my hand but they would not stand to the justice of Japan but would have their demand or not go forward in the voyage.'

On the 28th the merchants pressed Adams to pay the crew something on account, as a recognition of the hardships they had already endured. Adams sensing full well the danger of the situation, told them that he would have to be given stronger reasons than 'pitifulness and compassion', refused, and spent the next day trying to persuade some of his passengers 'to go in the room of mariners'. Fifty apparently agreed to do so but then backed down, whereupon Wickham as chief merchant swore roundly that there would be no voyage unless the ringleaders of the strike were put ashore and left behind. But the men remained unshaken by these threats and 'seeing there was no other remedy' it was agreed that half their wages should be advanced them, subject only to the face-saving condition that the final amount of their payment should be subject to official arbitration on their return to Japan.

Heavy rain delayed the reloading of ballast for a day and yet another day's delay was occasioned by a great procession and prayer-festival in the town, 'so this day passed with little furtherance of our business, the more was my grief'. Further storms held back the re-setting of the masts and a second confrontation with the crew seemed likely until the merchants persuaded Adams to stay his hand until Siam was reached — 'otherwise I could not proceed this year to which I seeing [this] to be most true, I consented unto, contrary to my will, God knoweth.'

By 11 February, water and provisions having been taken aboard, the *Sea Adventure* was ready to set sail but did not

Siamese image scroll and other religious ornaments that belonged to Adams.

Photograph of Anjin-cho, Tokyo, in about 1870, named after Adams and once the site of his home.

because the crew refused to give the merchants written receipts for the advance of their wages. A week of alternating storms and calms then followed, making sailing impossible anyway. Adams and Wickham and the others held long discussions as to whether they should put about for Japan at the first opportunity or wait for six months until the next favourable winds. Before they could come to a firm conclusion, however, it seemed as though the decision might be taken out of their hands as a messenger came from the local lord's court demanding to know whether the strangers intended to depart or to stay until the next monsoon. Playing for time, they replied that their decision would depend upon orders from their headquarters in Japan. Two days later the lord's messengers returned and asked them to wait out their time at Oshima because in three months a Chinese trading vessel would call and 'if we were here it would be an occasion to cause them to lose their trade which only they by their means did live upon'. Adams's response was both bold and diplomatic: 'I answered that I was but one [man]. I did not care whether I died in here or in the sea but I prayed to have compassion of... both passengers and mariners, about 120 or 130 persons and with this answer I did leave them, waiting for further answer from them.'

The blustery weather continued, delaying the departure of the ship's pinnace for Japan, in search of orders. Wickham meanwhile had a fight with Damian Marin, a Portuguese enlisted in the company's service. Adams, whose responsibilities evidently weighed heavily upon him, 'did no thing but walk melancholy and muse solitary'. With the passage of another fruitless week general gloom turned into general discontent and on 5 March a full-blown affray threatened to break out between the passengers and the crew. Lord Shobei, a Japanese merchant, charged into the market-place on shore at the head of twenty men armed with swords and pikes and bows and arrows. But Adams managed to head off a group of about forty sailors and, with the assistance of Wickham, 'did so persuade on both sides as there was no blood shed of no party, thanks be to almighty God, for ever, amen'.

It took more than a week to reconcile the two sides. On the day after the incident in the market-place Adams persuaded the would-be combatants not to carry long weapons, 'so this day passed without any further broil'. But three days later Shobei's men were still carrying swords. The arrival in due course of royal officials from the capital gave added weight to the unceasing efforts of the pilot and his companions to bring about a general peace. In the process Wickham and Damian made up their differences. On 22 March a local festival with 'cock-fighting and running of horses' finally brought a close to an ugly episode.

Two days later Adams received an invitation from the lord to visit him in his capital and attend a banquet. The pilot replied, with scant regard for diplomatic nicety, that if he could not get formal permission to wait out the summer at anchor 'the sight of the city was no pleasure to me'. On 26 March, it being Easter Sunday, the English had a celebration of their own and 'were very merry according to the time'. The festive spirit was not, however, general and 'he that had been the cause of the great mutiny being still full of desperate parts this night Shobei Dono killed him'. As if to mark his satisfaction with this turn of events the Japanese merchant then took himself off to a banquet in the capital.

After another week of bad weather and enforced idleness the crew again became restless and mischievous and on 6 April two of them were arrested for various misdemeanours. In the absence of the local magistrate, who was away in the capital, Adams could do nothing for several days to secure their release. Rainy, overcast weather continued and so did the crew's undisciplined behaviour. On 12 April, after a double earth-tremor, a sailor was seized by other members of the crew and accused of theft. They were for cutting him to pieces on the spot but Adams forbade it on the grounds that as they were about to return to Japan he should be dealt with there.

A week later he recorded that he had 'much ado with our men about their disorder ashore' and it took another ten days and the assistance of the local authorities to get them back on board ship. Adams also had to pay off all debts they had run up while ashore. A further week passed in loading up a cargo of wheat and heaving out ballast to keep the ship in trim. This operation bought its own troubles when Wickham accused Adams of secretly arranging with Damian Marin to sell half the wheat on their own rather than the company's account. Adams and Damian both denied the accusation in front of the other merchants and Wickham let the matter drop.

On 12 May came sudden and unexpected news. Ieyasu, then besieging Osaka Castle in a final struggle for power, had, it was said, suffered a great reverse and was 'like to lose his country'. Alarmed at the possibility of the fall of the ruler upon whom their trading rights depended, the English decided to delay their departure yet again and to seek confirmation of the news from some samurai recently arrived from Kyushu. Wickham made it very clear to Adams he would go alone to see them 'and as for me I should take no care he would do well enough without me, so I returned aboard'.

On 15 May local officials demanded to know why the *Sea Adventure* lay still at anchor although there was a fair wind for Japan. Adams reminded them stiffly that their lord was under Ieyasu's suzerainty, and that they were trying to put at risk the lives of more than one hundred people, but that nevertheless if it was the local ruler's will he would depart at the first opportunity. After another week of bad weather, and with no firm news either way regarding Ieyasu's fortunes, Adams finally put to sea on 21 May after a sojourn in Okinawa of almost six months. On 12 June after a short but unpleasant return journey he reached Kyushu and off-loaded his cargo of wheat at Kawachi harbour — 'thus, God have the praise, we ended our troublesome voyage.'

As a commercial venture the expedition had been a virtual disaster — 'it hath not pleased God that this year we should make any profit of our labour and trouble', as Wickham later put it. But it did have one beneficial outcome. Knowing him to be a keen gardener, Adams bought back for Cocks a strange root plant he had seen growing in the Ryukyus. And thus the sweet potato came to Japan.

16

'the fortres of Osekey'

'There came letters . . . that it is true that the emperor hath . . . taken the fortres of Osekey and entered into it . . . Fidaia Samme and his mother . . . having cut their bellies . . .'

DIARY OF RICHARD COCKS, 5 JUNE 1615

While Adams ventured to sail for Siam, Ieyasu moved to make himself master of Japan once and for all. In the decade after his victory over Ishida at Sekigahara he had strengthened his position in the country by building fortresses, by redistributing the lands of his defeated enemies to extend his network of grateful supporters and by increasing his own revenues. Death meanwhile had deprived Hideyori of many of his most staunch allies and protectors. As he entered the eighth decade of his life Ieyasu determined to destroy the house of Toyotomi.

He found a pretext by alleging that the inscription on a ceremonial bell cast at Hideyori's expense contained a pun on his name which was both threatening and insulting. As the summer of 1614 turned into autumn both sides prepared for war. Thousands of *ronin,* masterless samurai, flocked to Hideyori's stronghold at Osaka, eager to revenge themselves against the man who had despoiled their masters and cast them adrift. The English meanwhile did a brisk trade in munitions with both sides, raising the price of gunpowder 60 per cent between June and October.

Osaka Castle was undoubtedly the strongest fortress in Japan. Bounded on the west by the sea itself, it was also protected to the north by three rivers. The central keep stood within two moats and was surrounded by walls 120 feet high. The outer defences stretched for nearly nine miles. All the main gates were protected by cannon and there were fire-throwing mangonels stationed every few hundred yards along the walls. Supply, so often the weak point of a besieged garrison, had also been well taken care of. Enough food and ammunition had been stockpiled to enable the 90,000-strong garrison to fight for literally years on full rations.

Osaka Castle.

Against this formidable bastion Ieyasu brought a besieging army of 180,000 and his own matchless cunning. Early skirmishes soon showed that the defenders would put up the stiffest resistance and inflict very heavy casualties. Ieyasu, to Hidetada's annoyance, soon gave up the idea of a frontal assault and ordered an intimidating artillery bombardment to be launched at dawn and at ten o'clock at night for three consecutive days. Meanwhile sappers were set to work to undermine the castle's outermost towers.

After six weeks the attackers seemed no nearer their objective than when they had begun. Indeed, Ieyasu may have lost as much as a fifth of his forces by that time. And the severity of the winter imposed much hardship on his surviving troops. He therefore resorted to bribery, but the would-be traitor was discovered and beheaded; and a second attempt at the same stratagem was dismissed with loud and public contempt by a more principled defender.

At this point Ieyasu opted for subterfuge, dispatching a female envoy to negotiate terms with Hideyori's mother, whom he knew to be more than a little anxious to ensure the survival of her son. While the negotiations proceeded Ieyasu underlined the desirability of a settlement by keeping up a protracted artillery bombardment and parading 100,000 war-chanting samurai up and down ouside the castle walls.

These carrot-and-stick tactics paid dividends and Hideyori agreed to come to terms, swayed on the one hand by his mother's fears and on the other by the avarice of some of his leading supporters, who hoped to bargain back from the Tokugawa the lands they had forfeited after Sekigahara. Ieyasu offered a pardon for all Hideyori's garrison and freedom for their commander to live where he chose in Japan. In return they were to bind themselves not to raise another rebellion against his rule. The 'terrible old man' even signed the final articles of agreement with blood squeezed from his own hand.

The day after the terms were sealed, 22 January 1615, Ieyasu made a show of disbanding his forces by marching a contingent off to embark at the nearest harbour. The main body of his troops, however, were set to work immediately filling in the outer moat of Osaka Castle. Demolition of the fortifications had been mentioned during the negotiations with Hideyori but formed no part of the agreement which was sealed. On the other hand, if Hideyori had agreed to submit to Tokugawa suzerainty and foresworn all thoughts of rebellion, why should he need to shelter his loyalty and honest intentions behind walls and ditches?

By the time the Osaka commanders had mounted a formal protest the outer wall of the castle was in the outer moat, which had thus been obliterated. The protests were acknowledged and attended to — while the work of filling in the second moat went on apace. In less than a month, this, too, had disappeared and the defences of the fortress were reduced to a single moat and wall. When Hideyori then attempted to re-excavate the second moat Ieyasu accused him of breaking their agreement and moved against him with a new army of some 200,000 men.

Hideyori, now that his fortifications had been so gravely weakened, felt obliged to take the war to his enemy and sent raiding parties deep into Ieyasu's territory. But the decisive confrontation took place before Osaka Castle itself.

The plan of the Osaka garrison was in essence simple. One portion of their forces would attack the main Tokugawa army, aiming to engage it, but no more. Meanwhile a flying column would sweep round the battling armies and fall upon them from the rear. As it did so, the rest of the garrison, led by Hideyori himself, carrying Hideyoshi's famous standard, would sally from the castle to press home the attack from the front.

In the event, the first frontal attack by the Osaka troops was pressed too hard for the flying column to carry out its intended manoeuvre. Hideyori's men, however, fought with such ferocity that for a while the outcome of the battle seemed in doubt, the Tokugawa host being so vast that various units crashed into each other and moved with such poor coordination that cries of treachery went up as commanders misinterpreted the intentions of their comrades-in-arms. But eventually the sheer weight of numbers told and the Osaka troops found themselves pressed up against their own walls. An entry was at last forced by the attackers and fierce hand-to-hand fighting finally brought them to the inner citadel. Most of the castle was by now in flames and the fires continued throughout the night.

Accepting the hopelessness of his position, Hideyori, in the keep, committed suicide. His remains were never found and rumours circulated for years afterwards that he had been seen, a fugitive, in different parts of the country. Even if he had survived, further thoughts of rebellion would have been futile. Ieyasu had ensured the extinction of his line by executing his eight-year-old-son. And the heads of his supporters were rotting by the roadside all the way from Kyoto to Fushimi.

A sixteenth century suit of armour.

The destruction of Osaka Castle and the house of Toyotomi removed the last great obstacle to the definitive establishment of Tokugawa authority. Regulations were issued in August 1615 to govern the conduct of the nation's ruling samurai elite. They were enjoined to live frugally, to work diligently and to keep up their martial skills. Strict surveillance was to be kept over the construction of all fortifications and the arrangement of all aristocratic marriages, which might serve to cover potential alliances and conspiracies. Together with control of the major roads, ports and mines and a quarter of the country's agricultural output and most of its foreign trade, as well as an elaborate security system based on spies and hostages, these measures assured the pre-eminence of the Tokugawa dynasty for more than two and a half centuries. As Adams himself succinctly put it after the fall of Osaka Castle, 'Thus ended the wars.'

17

'in thear relligion veri zellous'

'In their religion very zealous, or superstitious, having divers sects, but praying all of them sects, to one saint . . .'
LETTER OF WILLIAM ADAMS, JANUARY 1613

Early missionary work in Japan had been virtually monopolized by Portuguese Jesuits, who followed a policy of assimilation to Japanese life-styles. In outward forms of dress, diet, speech and manners Jesuit missionaries strove diligently either to follow Japanese customs or at least not to behave in any way likely to disgust or outrage local opinion.

They were, from time to time, subjected to official harassment but nevertheless managed to maintain a momentum of conversion among both the poor and the powerful. Their dismay at the arrival of Spanish friars in 1593 can be imagined. The Franciscans, who came ostensibly as ambassadors from the Spanish colonial authorities in the Philippines, were as zealous as the Jesuits were subtle. Dissension soon became open and provoked the authorities into a sudden and terrible act of repression. In 1597 Hideyoshi ordered the execution of seven Franciscans and nineteen of their Japanese converts. Arrested in Kyoto, they were tortured and mutilated and then paraded, as a warning, until they came to Nagasaki, where they were crucified upside down, like common criminals. An order went out that all missionaries should leave Japan, except for a very few, who were to be allowed to remain to minister to the religious needs of Portuguese residents. Some did leave, but the vast majority went into hiding and continued their pastoral work under the protection of noble converts or by bribing petty officials.

The situation worsened after 1608 when the pope revoked the Portuguese monopoly on missionary work and the King of Spain followed suit by allowing Spaniards to trade with Japan henceforth. The arrival of first the Dutch and then the English increased the disunity of the Christian community. Their constant bickerings and

The Great Buddha of Kamkura dedicated in 1252.

mutual accusations of heresy, rebellion and subversion not unnaturally strengthened the feeling of the Japanese authorities that the alien religion might well become a serious threat, not merely to public order, but to the stability of the state itself.

Writing at about this time Adams emphasized both the mutual tolerance of the Buddhists and the increasing persecution directed against the Catholics. The Japanese were, he wrote, 'in their religion very zealous or superstitious, having divers sects, but praying all them sects, or the most part, to one saint, which they call Ameeda [i.e. Buddha], which they esteem to be their mediator between God and them; all these sects living in friendship one with another, not one against other, but every one as his conscience teacheth'. But the position of the 'many Christians of the Romish order' was far less enviable: 'in the year 1612 is put down all the sects of the Franciscans. The Jesuits have ... privilege ... being in Nagasaki, in which place only may so many as will of all sects: in other places not many permitted.'

From this time onwards royal displeasure against the Christians became unrelentingly severe. Writing in 1613 Saris recorded that 'the emperor being displeased with the Christians, made proclamation that they should forthwith remove and carry away all their churches to Nagasaki ... and that no Christian church should stand nor mass be sung, within ten leagues of his court, upon pain of death.' Saris also noted down one of the most astonishing of the many strange episodes which accompanied the persecution of a church increasingly forced underground:

'certain of the naturals [i.e. Japanese] being seven and twenty in number, men of good fashion, were assembled together in a hospital, appointed by the Christians for lepers, and there had a mass; whereof the emperor being informed, commanded them to be shut up in a house for one night, and that the next day they should suffer death. The same evening another man was locked up in the same house for debt, he being a heathen at his coming in and ignorant of Christ and his religion. But — which is wonderful — the next morning, when the officer called at the door for those which were Christians to come forth, and go to execution, and those which were not, and did renounce the same, to stay behind: this man, in that night's space, was so instructed by the others, that resolutely he came out with the rest, and was crucified with them.'

In January 1614 Ieyasu issued an edict suppressing Christianity in Japan. Churches in Kyoto were pulled down. Missionaries and some Japanese Christians of high rank were arrested and exiled.

Only a few of the common folk suffered for their faith, the main motive for the persecution apparently being the fear that the spread of Christianity among the samurai would undermine feudal loyalties and thus the key social relationship underlying the political order. Ieyasu's antagonism can only have been strengthened by the fact that Christians were numerous amongst Hideyori's supporters at the siege of Osaka Castle. This was certainly the impression of contemporaries, as a Jesuit chronicler of that bloody event recorded that 'there were so many crosses, Jesu's and Sant 'Iago's on their flags, tents and other martial insignia ... that this must needs have made Ieyasu sick to his stomach.'

Despite the severe terms in which the official disapproval of the foreign religion was proclaimed, many missionaries continued their activities quite openly. During Ieyasu's lifetime none were put to death, no doubt because the struggle for Osaka Castle commanded a higher place in his order of priorities.

Ieyasu died in June 1616, and under Hidetada all restraint was removed. A new edict of September 1616 banned all priests, including those previously allowed to serve the Portuguese merchants. Japanese were forbidden, under penalty of being burned alive and having all their property confiscated, even to give shelter to priests, their protectors or servants. The same penalties were to be applied to women, to children and to the five nearest neighbouring families of an offending household. Unusually, the proclamation was made not merely verbally but also by means of placards posted throughout the realm.

Cocks leaves us in no doubt of the virulence of Hidetada's hatred of Christianity: 'this emperor is a great enemy of the name of Christians, especially Japans, so that all which are found are put to death. I saw fifty-five martyred at Miyako [Kyoto] ... and amongst them were little children of five and six years old burned in their mothers' arms.... In the town of Nagasaki, there were sixteen more martyred ... whereof five were burned and the rest beheaded and cut in pieces, and cast into the sea in sacks ... yet the priests got them up again, and kept them secretly for relics. There is many more in prison in divers other places, as also here, which look hourly when they shall die, for very few turn pagans.'

Buildings, as well as people, were to be marked for destruction 'there were some remnants standing in Nagasaki till this year, and the monastery of Misericordia not touched, neither any churchyard, nor burial place, but now by order from the emperor all is pulled down, and all graves and sepulchres opened, and dead men's bones taken out, and carried into the fields by their parents and kindred to be buried elsewhere. And streets made in all their places, where the emperor hath commanded pagodas to be erected, and sent heathen priests to live in them, thinking utterly to root out the memory of Christianity out of Japan.'

When Hidetada learned that, despite these severities, attempts were still being made to smuggle priests into Japan, the persecutions reached new extremes of horror. The priests, the captain of the ship which brought them, its Christian crew and passengers were martyred. Three weeks later occurred the 'Great Martyrdom' at Nagasaki — thirty Christians were beheaded and twenty-five others, including nine foreign priests, roasted to death. According to a later account, 'all the bodies, with images, rosaries and all the objects of religion seized among the Christians, were cast together into a great pit, as pestiferous objects.... They threw into this pit... the stakes and... the ashes, a layer of bodies of the decapitated, a layer of wood, then they piled on all the objects of religion and set fire to the mass. It burned for two days. Then they collected the ashes, and even the earth soaked with the blood shed. The ashes of this earth were put into straw sacks and they were sent to be scattered on the open sea. Afterwards the boatmen were made to strip and bathe, to wash the bags and even the boats, so that no dust or any vestige might remain after this great holocaust.'

By 1629 it had become customary to force suspected Christians to tread on an image of the crucifixion or the virgin and child to prove their abjuration of the faith. Those who refused were tortured into apostasy or, if obdurate, executed. The persecution came to its dreadful climax in 1637 when 20,000 peasants, oppressed by exorbitant local taxes, rose against their lords, carrying Christian symbols and singing hymns. For three months they held the old castle on the Shimabara peninsula in western Kyushu against the shogun's army. The rebels were, with the aid of a Dutch naval bombardment, crushed and massacred. The following year all Japanese were forced to register at local Buddhist temples as believers. The preaching of Christianity was forbidden for almost 250 years.

18

'com againe to morrow'

'And after noon Capt. Adames and our jurebasso went again to the court and saw all the council together, who gave them fair words as before, bidding them come again tomorrow.'
DIARY OF RICHARD COCKS, 12 OCTOBER 1616

In July 1615, shortly after his return from the Ryukyus, Adams found himself drawn into a particularly unpleasant quarrel. Gorezano, an interpreter hired by Cocks, had, it was alleged, slandered the brother-in-law of Lord Yasemon, at whose house Adams habitually stayed while in Hirado. Gorezano, whom later experience proved to be both treacherous and vindictive, denied the charge. Cocks, inexperienced in the ways of the Japanese, and half-believing the interpreter to be the innocent victim of a devious Dutch ploy to create trouble for the English, 'was glad to send Capt. Adams to take up the matter'.

Japanese accusers demanded that the interpreter should be dismissed by Cocks and made to leave town forthwith. Cocks bluntly reminded them that he and the members of his household were under the specific protection of the shogun. This veiled threat 'put them into such a quandary that they sent me word that, for my sake, they were content to pardon him of all matters and to be his friend'. (In fact they beat him up one dark night a couple of weeks later.) Cocks noted in his diary that 'this word was sent me per Capt. Adames' but, far from setting down any words of gratitude to him for his role as mediator, he set down at considerable length his suspicions of the pilot: 'whom, before God and man, I must needs blame for taking part with that vile fellow ... Lord Yasemon, whom, per experience I have found to be an absolute cunning knave, and thereupon have done all I can to make Capt. Adames to know it; yet he still esteemeth him more than all our English nation, and still he would pawn his life and soul for his honesty. And I cannot choose but note it down ... that he is much more friend to the Dutch than to the Englishmen, which are his own countrymen, God forgive him.'

Cocks also believed Lord Yasemon to have profited secretly from the sale of an over-priced junk to the East India Company but conceded that 'Capt. Adames have no hand in the matter. For with their smooth speeches they make a child of him and so do what they list, and he will not believe any man that will speak to the contrary.'

The chief merchant's suspicions of Adams were further strengthened at the beginning of September when the pilot received a sudden summons to hurry to Ieyasu's court. 'I suspect it was a plot laid before by Capt. Adams himself and the Dutch, to the intent he might go up to serve their turns ... or else it may be he seeketh occasion to get the emperor to command him to stay and not to proceed forward to the Siam voyage, his time of service to the Company being out within two months.' Adams, who was in fact genuinely surprised at the summons, volunteered the theory that the ex-shogun might be anxious for information about a newly built fortress in the Ryukyus which might serve as a possible base for the defeated supporters of Hideyori to regroup in. In fact they were both wrong.

Whatever the cause, Adams's imminent departure could not have come at a more awkward time from Cocks's point of view, for it coincided with the arrival of an English ship, the *Hoseander*, and Cocks had decided that its commander, Captain Coppindale, should pay his respects to Ieyasu at his court. In the event, Adams, Coppindale, Eaton and Wickham all left together, though Adams raced ahead of his companions several times on the journey in an attempt to catch up with the peripatetic ex-shogun. When they did gain audience of Ieyasu he professed himself delighted with the presents they brought and gave them gifts of clothes and weapons in return.

Adams's status as the trusted aide of Japan's ruler was emphasized in the eyes of his countrymen when he was dispatched on Ieyasu's behalf to Uraga where a delegation of friars from New Spain had landed. (This had been the purpose of the mysterious summons.) Adams's task was to inform them that neither their presents nor their persons were any longer welcome in Japan. Given his past experience of the Jesuits and their attitudes towards him as a Protestant, this chore may not have been entirely distasteful to him.

Despite this detour Adams managed to arrive back at Hirado before Coppindale and the others. And, as if finally to underline his indispensability, he brought with him an order from Ieyasu to the

Portuguese in Nagasaki to release Damian Marin and Juan de Lievana, whom they had imprisoned and sentenced to death for accepting employment with the English.

No sooner had he arrived back at Hirado than the pilot set off for Siam, again in the *Sea Adventure*. The voyage, apart from a great gale which washed the ship's pump overboard, was uneventful. The fact that the junk coped with 'sea coming in on both sides' was a tribute to Adams's efforts in seeing that it was 'strong and well repaired'.

In Siam, after the customary present-giving and bribery, they bought such large quantities of wood and skins that they had to charter two extra junks to bring the whole cargo back. All three did eventually get back to Japan, although one junk did so only after a most hazardous voyage which claimed the lives of its Japanese captain and many of its crew. The venture did, however, prove to be an enormously profitable one. The cargo of the *Sea Adventure* was sold for double what it cost. Indeed, it was the single most successful enterprise conducted by the English factory in Japan in the entire ten years of its existence.

When Adams returned to Hirado he found another English ship, the *Advice*, at anchor at the harbour. He also learned that in his absence his long-time patron Ieyasu had at last died and been succeeded by Hidetada, now ruler of Japan in fact as well as name. Cocks judged the occasion timely for another visit to court, so once again Adams found himself accompanying the English party on the wearisome trek to Edo.

After more than three weeks on the road the travellers were delighted to find themselves met by tenants from Adams's estate at Hemi bearing welcome baskets of fresh European-style food — bread, boiled beef and wine. Adams then rode ahead to Edo to prepare his house in Nihonbashi, where the English were to reside during their stay in the shogun's capital. The next morning he greeted them at the city gates and escorted them into the city.

Three days later Cocks presented himself before Hidetada. Both the setting and the occasion made a deep impression upon him. He estimated that there were more than 10,000 people in and around the castle, which he judged to be 'very strong ... and a league over each way'. The shogun's palace itself was 'huge ... all the rooms being gilded' except where the walls were covered with paintings of exotic wild animals such as 'lions, tigers ... panthers, eagles'. While high court officials waited respectfully outside, Cocks and his two companions were admitted to the ruler's presence. They

Yukata featuring the fifty-three stages of the Tokaido.

found him sitting 'cross-legged like a tailor' on a low dais. Well-briefed by Adams, Cocks stood his ground when bidden to approach nearer. This conformity to the hidden understandings of court etiquette 'as I understood afterwards, was well esteemed of'. After a few minutes the visitors were dismissed by a slight nod of the shogun's head, the entire meeting having passed in complete silence.

This was well begun but a week later Adams, after daily attendance at court, had still not received any written confirmation that the trading privileges enjoyed by the English under Ieyasu would be continued under his successor. To his alarm he was informed by a court official that word had reached Edo that his wife was sheltering priests in his house at Hemi. (In fact they may have been Spanish merchants.) 'So Capt. Adames sent away an express with a letter to his wife to look to it that there were no such matter,' Hidetada having but recently issued an edict 'That no padres be found amongst them and them in whose houses they are found shall be put to death with all their generation'. Two days later Adams 'wrote again to his folks to look out that no such matter were proved against them, as they tendered their lives'.

Cocks then 'got Capt. Adames to go ... to the Emperor's secretary ... to give him to understand ... that we are no friends of the Jesuits or friars, neither suffer any of their sect to remain in England, but punish all them which are found with death; this course having been kept in England for above the space of sixty years, so that the emperor need not fear our conversation with that sect, for that their hatred against us and our religion was more than against any others whatsoever'.

Adams's speech seems to have had the desired effect because, after a further entirely superfluous warning to have nothing to do with Catholic priests, he was told not to be dismayed by the length of time it was taking to deal with his request.

After ten more daily attendances Adams at last secured the longed-for document. Cocks later learned that much of the delay had been caused by the interpreter Gorezano, who, antagonized against Adams by his support for Yasemon Dono the previous year, had put it about the court that the pilot had dissuaded the English merchants from bringing more lavish gifts than those which they actually presented.

To celebrate their success the English party went off to Adam's estate to the south for a short holiday. Here they saw him play the part of the grand seigneur, with dozens of local people running in front of his horse for eight or nine miles at the time 'as homagers'. At Hemimura Cocks and his companions were treated with royal hospitality, but the mood of euphoria was soon broken by the arrival of an express letter from Wickham at Hirado, bearing news of a proclamation that no Japanese should buy goods from foreign merchants in Kyoto, Osaka and Sakai. If this proved true it would mean the abandonment of the network of agencies which had been so painstakingly established.

Cocks, Eaton and Adams therefore returned post-haste to Edo to clarify the situation. It was soon confirmed by a high official that the English might continue to trade in Hirado but nowhere else. Cocks was as angry as he was depressed:

'I answered him that the emperor might as well banish us right out of Japan as bind us to such an order, for that we could make no sales at that place, as I had found by experience of three years' space and upwards.... He answered me that he could not withstand the emperor's pleasure and that at present all matters were in other manner in Japan than in time of the old emperor.'

A further ten days attendance at court brought nothing but fair words and a final confirmation that Hidetada's decision could not be reversed for at least a year, the orders having been published. As a special concession the English were to be allowed to sell off, through Japanese agents, the goods they had stockpiled around the country. Cocks handed this chore over to Adams, although his two-year contract with the Company was nearly at an end.

On the way back to Hirado Adams dislocated his shoulder in falling from his horse, which reared up suddenly when a startled bird flew out of a wayside hedge. Cocks thought Adams very lucky — '1,000 to 1 that he had not broke his neck'. As it was he was laid up at an inn for four or five days, rejoining the others when they reached Kyoto, 'yet not without pain in his shoulder'. The party eventually arrived back at Hirado on 4 December after an absence of five months. Almost the sole constructive achievement of the enterprise was Cocks's decision to sack Gorezano en route. Idle, abusive and deceitful, 'this Gorezano had been a dead man long ago', Cocks wrote disgustedly in his diary, 'if I had not spared him, and have this reward for my labour.'

A week after his return Adams found himself once again in conflict with Cocks over allegations of dishonesty on the part of two of his Japanese associates. Cocks, writing as it were between clenched teeth, set it down in his diary that 'I take God to witness I do what I can to keep in with this man.' After another week had passed good relations seem to have been restored, Adams inviting all the English to a banquet, complete with strolling players for their after-dinner entertainment. A fortnight later Cocks sold Adams one of the Company's junks for little more than half what it had cost.

19

'but a loosing voyage'

*'Before dinner Ed. Sayer... brought me in a letter from Capt. Adames
... advising he hath found but a losing voyage.'*
DIARY OF RICHARD COCKS, 7 AUGUST 1617

The year 1617 found Adams sailing once more. His voyage had two major objectives — to establish regular trading relations with Cochin-China (Vietnam) and to solve the mystery of the 1614 disappearance of Tempest Peacock, his companion Walter Carwardine and his cargo. The first object was more or less achieved, the second was not.

The voyage began inauspiciously. Adams's half-priced junk, *The Gift of God*, named for one of the ships in his Armada supply fleet, was held in harbour by contrary winds. The delay this occasioned, unfortunately for the pilot, gave some relatives of the local daimyo their chance to take the law into their own hands over a dispute they had had with Adams regarding their shares in the cargo of timber he had brought back from Siam on his previous voyage. They were no doubt encouraged by the knowledge that Adams had just been reproved by the local daimyo for failing to use his carpenters in fitting out the junk for sea and had therefore forfeited his protection. Bounding aboard, the angry Japanese set upon the startled Englishmen, wrenching Adams's arms almost out of their sockets, seizing Sayers, the chief merchant, by the hair, and threatening the boatswain with a knife. Adams saved them from a severe beating by taking out the shogun's travel documents, kissing them ostentatiously and waving them above his head. This rather theatrical gesture reminded his persecutors that they were dealing with a man who had direct access to the highest in the land. They therefore desisted and Adams, to avoid further delay, decided to make no complaint against them.

The voyage itself lasted a little under a month and was relatively uneventful. But the final approaches to their destination proved awkward to negotiate. They were delayed first by a great storm, which the junk rode out at anchor, and then by shoals, which could only be passed at full tide. Having entered the river they sought, the voyagers were then beset by another gale which broke the ship's flagstaff and, more important, two hawsers, and then finally beached her. Adams's log-book entry for the day then closes with the dry observation that 'we could not get her off till the flood, so this day passed with labour enough.'

The welcome ashore was, however, more promising. Edmund Sayers was 'well entertained' by the two sons of 'dackeedono', a leading member of the resident Japanese trading community. The next day the man himself appeared and told Sayers that the local ruler was delighted to receive English traders and would extend to them every facility and protection. A few days later Sayers and Adams had an important interview with the king's secretary. They explained that they came, in Adams's words, 'to know his pleasure whether ... we might have free trade in his country and also to know what offence our men ... had committed that they were killed; if they had done any offence against the King or his laws their death was no matter but if without offence, to seek justice ...'

Sayers records the official's suspiciously evasive reply that 'the King did not know of the killing of them but they were drowned by mischance in a small boat, but said he, that is gone and past, it is not needful for to speak of this now' and his equally unconvincing assurances that 'you shall have new ingress here in this country, he swearing by the all mighty God and whatsoever he would request for a trade into the country, I should not fear but he would do it all himself with the king'. He then changed tack and accused the missing Peacock of having 'given many scornful speeches and proud, not making any reckoning of the King nor his country, saying that they could if they wished not suffer any junks to come thither, whether Japanese or Chinese, which did go very near them, he being a stranger and to give such proud speeches in their own country'.

Nevertheless it was agreed that the English party should go up to the court very shortly to hand over gifts and obtain written confirmation of trading rights.

When Sayers and Adams went back the next day, however, they were told that the journey to the king's court should be postponed, it being a 'great journey and too much pains for us to take'. The Englishmen protested that the beginning of an important new trading relationship merited every possible effort on their part and that they dared not return to Japan without having seen the king in person. This protest won them promise of further enquiries and they broke off the interview with a reminder to their hosts that if they should come to any harm their countrymen would certainly know of it.

On the following day Sayers and Adams were again subjected to a barrage of discussion, which confirmed their suspicion that the official was himself deeply implicated in the death of Peacock and feared that if the Englishmen should raise the matter at court his role would be revealed. (Further confirmation came later when the Japanese man who had acted as host to Peacock and was known to be very close to the local officials suddenly disappeared, to be heard of no more.) For a while they attempted to call his bluff, threatening to go unless detained by main force, but eventually they prudently accepted the advice of 'dackeedono' and agreed that he should accompany the official to court with their gifts and letters. Doubtless they were gratified by his assurance that once the king had received these evidences of their good intentions he would not fail to send for them when they came the following year and that such a direct summons could not be impeded by the interference of one of his subordinate officers.

A fortnight later the Englishmen received from the king encouraging words of welcome and protection, gifts of cloth and an enquiry 'why we did not come to him ourselves, for he would fain have seen us, we making answer to him he knew it was his own fault'. A few days afterwards the king let it be known that in return for a brass English cannon he would waive all future customs duties. That such a high value should be placed on a single powerful weapon would probably not have puzzled the visitors, who had by now begun to accumulate some first-hand knowledge of the violence prevalent in the country. Even as they began to trade, preparatory to their departure, news came that the agent of a Japanese merchant and two local men whom he had hired had been murdered and robbed on the road between the port and the capital.

Sayers bought all the silk he could from some Chinese traders and then, having cash to spare and not knowing what else to buy, was delighted when his interpreter brought along a Chinese and some samples which he said came from a large cargo of silk carried by the master of a Chinese junk then in harbour. Despite the high prices quoted Sayers leaped at the offer and, having weighed out virtually all his surplus fund into a bag, which was then carefully sealed, accompanied the interpreter to a reed hut to await delivery of his silk. Here he was warned to take great care of his money and put it behind his back, next to the wall, so that no one should see it. The interpreter and his Chinese friend then left, the latter to collect the silk and the former to go into his own hut, which just happened to adjoin the one in which Sayers sat waiting for the next hour. Fearing some mishap the Englishman at last rose to investigate the non-appearance of his expected goods, only to find his bag of money gone and a ragged hole in the wall which separated the Chinese go-betweens' hut from the interpreters'. Sayers ran to appeal to the head of the Chinese trading community for advice. He confirmed that the interpreter's Chinese friend had no silk to sell but counselled a philosophical attitude, assuring Sayers that the culprit would be caught and restitution made. With this assurance Sayers was obliged to rest content, Adams having readied the junk for the voyage home.

The voyage proved to be a rough one, the ship encountering a typhoon, 'the wind changing into all the points of the compass in twenty-four hours'. But, having endured 'an exceeding tempest of thunder and lightning, wind and rain', accompanied by eerie manifestations of St. Elmo's fire, the *Gift of God* at last came safely to harbour.

Adams could report with some satisfaction to Cocks that 'the King of Cochin-China is well contented our nation shall trade into his country'. Nevertheless, he had also to admit that in immediately commercial terms the venture had been 'but a losing voyage'.

20

'much adoe'

'No small trouble and grief . . . I having much ado to please all and yet cannot.'
DIARY OF RICHARD COCKS, 16 JANUARY 1618

No sooner had Adams stepped ashore from his 'losing voyage' than he found himself thrust into the middle of an ugly dispute. Nine days before his arrival fifteen Japanese seamen who had sailed to England with Saris four years earlier finally arrived back in Hirado. They claimed before Cocks that much money was still owed them in back-pay and that what they had already received was merely a bounty and no part of their wages. Hoping to find an ally in Adams, they appealed to him to intervene on their behalf. When he refused to be drawn into the quarrel, 'one of them took Captain Adames by the throat in his own lodging, because he would not stand out for them. . . .'

The pilot was no doubt pleased to leave Hirado a week later and accompany Cocks to court. The journey proved unpleasant thanks to foul weather and a bout of food-poisoning which afflicted both the English quite badly. Adams travelled in his own junk and came close to disaster — 'a leak springing in his bark, wetting and spoiling all his goods', Adams may well have felt himself dogged by continual misfortune, 'she being ready to sink under them.' It is perhaps significant that in the same paragraph in which he records this incident Cocks refers to Adams as 'the old man'.

The major object of the English embassy was 'to have our privileges enlarged that were shortened the year past'. As the English arrived, a Dutch embassy departed, having failed in the same enterprise. Undeterred, Cocks dispatched Adams to undertake the usual preparatory enquiries and present-giving and to hand over a second letter from King James of England. But despite a lavish distribution of gifts, progress was unexpectedly slow. On 19 September Cocks recorded in his diary that 'Capt. Adames went again this morning to the court, being returned yesternight with answer he should come again this morning, he having sat there all yesterday from morning till night without eating anything, as he had done the like the day before.'

At last, on 23 September:

'Capt. Adames returned from the Court with answer from the council that the emperor would give our English nation no larger privileges than other strangers have, only to sell our merchandise at Firando [Hirado] and Langasaque [Nagasaki]. The reason he doth it is for that his own merchants of Japan shall have the profit of selling within land before strangers, as also that, under colour of buying and selling, no priests may lurk up and down his country to alter religion, as hereto before they have done.'

Cocks took the implications of his reply pessimistically and 'advised Mr. Wickham ... to ... use diligence to sell something, for that we shall not be suffered to stay long after the emperor is departed'. Adams, meanwhile, persevered at court, seeking permissions for voyages to Cochin-China and Siam. These were finally supplied after a further week of waiting and supplication, but King James's letter was returned unanswered — 'the Emperor sent ... word that he would make no answer to the King of England's letter, nor send present, it being directed to his deceased father, a thing held ominous in Japan.' The final version of the trading privileges also omitted the right to sell at Nagasaki which had first been granted.

The pilot's persistence was rewarded by Cocks with presents for his wife, children and sister-in-law, Adams himself being next employed in a number of commercial negotiations with various officials and merchants, including the governor of Sakai, within whose jurisdiction Cocks wished to buy a quantity of firearms for export. There was a general ban on foreigners buying war material, for security reasons, but Cocks submitted that 'we brought better guns into Japan than we carried out, and that we did not buy these to weaken their country, nor to arm their enemies but were sent to their friends, and that I cared not much whether we had them or no.' Wickham was unable to get an audience of the governor to put forward these arguments but Adams, although he was also told that the governor was too ill to see anyone, did at least receive 'word about buying guns and armours, it was a thing forbidden per the emperor in respect of the Koreans, yet, notwithstanding, our host or others, by three or four at a time, might provide them, and he would not take knowledge thereof'.

Adams then remained in Osaka to wind up the Company's

business there, a necessary consequence of the failure to reverse the restriction of its trade privileges, and to collect as many outstanding debts as possible. Cocks meanwhile went forward to Hirado having sent word to the chief Chinese merchant there that Adams wished to sell off the *Gift of God*. This sale was eventually completed at 20 per cent more than the first offer made by the Chinese and so Adams received about the correct market value — which was about twice what he had paid for the leaky junk in the first place. Adams returned the favour by squeezing out some, but by no means all, of the money owed to the Company by its various debtors.

Even if the Company was experiencing difficulties in the conduct of business no one in the English factory at Hirado could complain that life was uneventful. The events of December 1617 must suffice to illustrate the pleasures and dangers of the world in which Cocks and his associates, including, of course, the indispensable Adams, were obliged to operate. On the first day of the month Cocks invited the local Chinese merchants over to a banquet — to eat up the left-overs from a banquet given to the Dutch the night before ('So it cost not much.'). On the 7th word came that the local daimyo's secretary had been ordered to hand over the profits of an illicit deal with the Dutch — 'or else to cut his belly' — and the luckless official 'not having it to pay, did it'. On the same day Cocks's knavish ex-interpreter Gorezano was, for like reason, commanded 'to get him out of the country with one suit of apparel on his back, and leave house, wife and children, and all the rest he hath, behind him'. A former favourite of the daimyo also suffered the same fate. On the 9th the local mint-master came to make arrangements to cast some of the Company's hoard of bullion into coin and on the same day Cocks interceded — successfully — with the local Dutch commander on behalf of three soliders condemned to the galleys for theft. More dining with the Dutch followed. Then on the 16 December, the Company's junk being about to depart for Siam, Japanese officials demanded that she take fourteen passengers along with her, despite the fact that Cocks 'had it under their hands to the contrary that they should carry none'. Eventually Cocks agreed to take seven as extra deck-hands — 'but know not whether they will be content therewith or no. God bless me out of the hands of these people.' That same day, as if Cocks had not enough to attend to, 'Mr. Totton fell into a strange humour, misusing Mr. Nealson in vile terms, telling me he was used like a slave in the English house, and, therefore, would come in it no more. This he did being in drink . . .'

A week later Adams at last returned from his debt-collecting, just in time to witness a memorable send-off for 'the Hollands general', bound for the Moluccas. Cocks being indisposed, Adams, Wickham and others were sent to represent him at the final departure of the Dutch ship. According to custom a salute of five guns was fired off, 'one of which pieces . . . being double charged by mischance, broke and staved five or six cabins and as many chests . . . and wounded and maimed seven or eight men, but none slain, and was in great danger to have fired all the gunpowder, being 200 barrels; which caused the fiscal, Mr. Albartus and the secretary to leap overboard into the sea. Two of them, not being able to swim, had like to have been drowned, and the third fell into a Japan boat, and . . . had like to have broken his legs. Yet in the end all turned into a laughter and mocking of those three men. And so gave the English kind entertainment.'

When they got back that night they learned that Wickham's new servant, a Japanese whom Cocks had recently saved from a death sentence, had stolen a silver cup from the Dutch house and sold it in the town. Cocks recovered and returned the stolen property, and saw to the culprit's punishment the following day, 'all the servants in the house, with others appointed, giving him ten lashes with a double rope over a naked body and buttocks, till the skin was beaten off, and after washed him in brine'. This, it must be remembered, was a gentle justice, compared to what a Japanese would have received at the hands of his countrymen — a death sentence.

The next day was Christmas, and there was a grand dinner for all the officers of the various ships and junks in the harbour, the Chinese captain coming with seasonal gifts of a fat capon, a basket of pears and ten boxes of marmalade. But whatever Yuletide cheer there might have been was dissipated in the following week by continuing wrangles over the question of taking Japanese passengers aboard the *Sea Adventure* to Siam, which caused the ship to lose a favourable wind.

Throughout the first three months of the new year Adams continued to work actively on the Company's behalf, although no longer technically in its employ. Indeed his assistance was now more valuable than ever, for his status as an honorary Japanese nobleman enabled him to pass off as his own the goods held in provincial warehouses which the Company was now forbidden to sell. Cocks also pressed Adams to accept a commission to act as pilot on the voyage to Cochin-China on behalf of a Chinese merchant from Nagasaki, the East India Company naturally hoping to share in the venture. Some evidence of Cocks's dependence on Adams can be seen in the pilot's handling of a dispute between himself and a Japanese merchant, 'Lord Gorobei', who appealed to Adams, accusing Cocks of false dealing. According to Cocks's own account, 'Capt. Adames fell into extreme terms... about Lord Gorobei... taking his part against me and all the English. I never saw him in the like humour.' Cocks backed down despite his firm conviction that he had been cheated by a forger and liar. Two days later Adams agreed to take on the Chinese merchant's commission.

Adams, accompanied by Sayers, set sail on 17 March after Cocks had thrown a send-off party, complete with dancing bears. The voyage was to prove completely abortive. The day after leaving the coast of Japan the junk was driven back and, in making harbour, struck a rock so hard that her rudder was severely damaged and stern-post smashed. The junk was unloaded and, with much labour, a new stern-post made and fitted. Bad weather delayed a fresh start and when it was made 'a great sea and a storm of wind' split the rudder so badly that Adams decided to run for the Ryukyus. Having obtained permission from the local authorities the crew cut down a tree to make a new rudder. But the tree proved to be rotten in the middle and so did a second. After protracted discussions it was determined that there was no practical option but to return to Japan. The continuing foul weather and the news that the *Sea Adventure* had also been forced back by contrary winds and a bad leak were no doubt also influential factors in forcing the adventurers to this conclusion. On 14 May Adams and his company returned to Hirado.

21

'from tooth outward'

'He told me that he noted a long time that the Hollanders and we were friends but from tooth outward and not cordially, as neighbours and friends ought to be.'
DIARY OF RICHARD COCKS, 3 JULY 1617

Relations between the English and the Dutch in Japan were at the same time both tense and intimate. The keenest of rivals in commerce, they were also well aware of their common vulnerability in a remote country whose customs were often incomprehensible and whose government was frequently capricious. They entertained one another with gusto and assisted each other in personal adversities and sickness. But Cocks's diary affords many instances of the suspicion and animosity which the one group held towards the other. Sometimes the cause was commercial sharp practice: 'I think the Hollanders play the geminies and go underhand to buy the timber when it is at the lowest.' Sometimes it was more serious: 'the Hollanders in all their thievish proceedings [i.e. privateering] give it out they are English.' National self-esteem was also a cause of dissension. Cocks boldly assured a puzzled Japanese nobleman that ill-feeling between the English and the Dutch was entirely the fault of the latter:

'I answered him the fault was not ours but the pride of the other, which would make the world to believe they were that which they were not. For that it was well known there was no comparison to be made betwixt their small state ... with the mighty and powerful government of the King of England, who did in some sort govern them, keeping garrisons in their chiefest places.'

The English were also wary of being identified in the eyes of the Japanese with the often disorderly behaviour of the Dutch 'It is strange to see the unruliness of these Holland Mariners and soldiers, how they go staggering drunk up and down the streets, slashing and cutting off each other with their knives, like madmen.'

Rumours also came to English ears that Dutch forces had

murdered Englishmen who had tried to claim territories in the Moluccas in the name of King James. Rumours were not proof but Cocks wrote down a careful account of the matter as it was reported to him, 'that whether I live or die, yet I hope this my handwriting may come to the hands of our honourable employers, and that our gracious sovereign, King James, will not let his subjects be murdered and his possessions taken from him in such sort'.

By 1618 the Dutch had established a fearsome reputation — in January of that year Adams reported to Cocks that the pilot of a ship from the Portuguese-controlled island of Macao had, at the mere sight of a Dutch ship, turned tail and run for the safety of Nagasaki harbour 'for fear she would have set upon her'. In June Cocks learned confidentially from the chaplain of the Dutch ship *Son*, who was an Englishman born in Hornchurch, Essex, that the Dutch had taken many Chinese junks off the coast of Vietnam. The Dutch made no mention of this to Cocks but suggested that all their raids had been directed against the Spanish in Manila. Thanks to his secret informant Cocks knew better and noted in his diary that 'people begin to murmur against the Hollanders for taking all junks they meet, whether they trade into Japan or no, and do all under the name of English. So God knoweth what will come of it.'

Nevertheless, the English continued to help the Dutch tow their ships into harbour, to exchange gifts with them and to entertain them hospitably.

Cocks, was, however, quite aware that the Dutch were abusing the protection afforded them in Japan. It was one thing for merchant ships to fight when they ran across the enemy on the high seas, quite another to patrol main shipping lanes and coastal waters for that very purpose. He therefore recorded that it was 'thought the emperor will bring matters in question, because these ... ships went out of purpose to rob and for nothing else, making by this means his country a receptacle of thieves, to his great dishonour and their own enriching. ... Spaniards, Portingales and Chinas will go to court and cry out with open mouth against them touching that matter. ... Because the emperor will not suffer his own vassals of Japon to do the like.'

As yet, though, Cocks appears to have had no thought of associating the English with any such protest and, indeed, two days after making the above entry in his diary he 'visited the Hollanders at their house, who used me very friendly' and admired their new warehouses, arsenal, dovecote and wharf. Less than a week later, however, he was confiding to his diary that the Dutch were making a great show of saluting their newly arrived shipping 'that they might laugh at us the better ... who, although they speak us fair, love us not. Yet I doubt not before it be long to see them fall into the trap they provide for others.' But only a few days after this, having been told in confidence by a Chinese merchant that the Dutch were ill-regarded by the shogun, the Spanish and Portuguese having brought up the old charge against them of being rebels against their rightful ruler, Cocks set it down as his considered opinion that 'if the Hollanders be driven out of Japan, the English must not stay behind' because to the Japanese 'we were all one in effect, although different in our proceedings'.

In mid-July word reached Cocks that 'the Hollanders misuse our English men in vile sort and take them prisoners in all places where they can lay hands on them'; yet he still felt able to accept a gift from the Dutch of 'five pieces China linen to make shirts of' and to raise no objection when Adams proposed to accompany a Dutch delegation to the shogun's court with the aim of trying to recover some of their former good standing in his eyes. Cocks, indeed, simply appears to have accepted that the pilot was 'now bound up with the Hollanders' and therefore decided to take advantage of his journey by using him as a postman, giving him no less than twelve letters to deliver en route.

A week after Adams's departure Cocks heard of the imminent arrival of a ship of unknown nationality. To his astonishment it turned out to be an English ship — brought in by the Dutch as a prize! Cocks at once abandoned his former policy and wrote an indignant letter to the Chinese at Nagasaki, offering to join them in any protest they might be making before the shogun. Then, having seen the captured ship towed into harbour 'in a bravado' with all guns blazing, he gave a very frosty reception to the interpreter sent across by the embarrassed Jacques Specx, the head of the Dutch factory, to offer up the ship and its contents. Twice the messenger was turned away, until at last Specx came himself 'using many complimentary words'. Cocks was sure that the prize had been thoroughly stripped and therefore regarded the offer of her return as a very threadbare gesture. Specx for his part pleaded that the local Dutch community had had no part in the matter and that even those who had taken the ship were only acting under orders. This drew a most scornful and stinging rebuke from the irate Englishman — 'why then, it seems your masters command you to be common thieves, to rob English, Spanish, Portingalles, Chinas, Javas and all others whatsoever, without respect.' Somewhat shaken, the Dutch protested that 'hitherto they had held friendship with us and still would do, till their commanders gave them order to the contrary'. This protestation won from Cocks only the dismissive observation that 'they might show themselves friends to the English, if they pleased either now or hereafter, but for my part I did not care a half-penny whether they did or no.'

The day following this unseemly exchange the English decided that Cocks should protest in person before the shogun against the Dutch. For this to be at all effective Adams's services would of course be essential and therefore 'it was ordained to send away a post, both by water and land, after Capt. Adames, to inform him of the thievery of the Hollanders, to the intent he should retire himself from them ... and not go with them before the emperor.'

A fortnight later Cocks set off for Edo. After a week on the road he was astounded to receive from Adams 'such an unseasonable and unreasonable letter as I little suspected he would have done, saying he was none of the Company's servant and is, as it seemeth, altogether Hollandized, persuading me not to go up about this matter'. More likely it was simply that Adams, with a better grasp of current court politics, knew that protest would be futile and possibly counter-productive. Hidetada was simply not interested in what went on outside his domain. But Cocks was not to be so easily deterred and pressed on with his 'long and troublesome voyage'. A month later, nearing their destination, the English party ran into the Dutch delegation, heading back from Edo towards Hirado. 'There was a small greeting betwixt us,' Cocks recorded drily.

Adams, having diplomatically let the Dutch get ahead of him, met Cocks and his companions on the road next day. Later the same day, Adams's children met the party outside the city with baskets of food. The day after that Adams went to court to ask for an audience for the English. Two days later he was summoned to receive an answer, 'but he remained there from noon till night and had not word spoken to him'. Two days after that he was told he had been granted an audience, but with Iemitsu, Hidetada's son, and not with the shogun himself. When the English delegation came to court, however, they were told to leave their presents but given no audience. Over the succeeding few days more presents were given to court officials and Adams continued to wait patiently, but to no effect, on Cocks's behalf. After a fortnight of such attendance the only acknowledgement he received was 'a nod and smiling countenance'. The contrast with his easy access in the days of Ieyasu could hardly have been greater.

Adams himself certainly seems to have become edgy and irritable. When one of Cocks's assistants, trying to tidy up some old outstanding business, asked him to hand over some unframed maps which company accounts indicated were still in his possession, Adams, according to Cocks, 'fell into such a chafe about that matter, telling them which were about him, in the Japan tongue, that this was not the first time we had charged him with false accounts.... Truly I was ashamed to hear him in such a humour; yet, after it seemed he recanted, for he came to me and asked if I knew of any such matter, and I answered him it appeared by Mr. Eaton's account that he had them.... So he went away and said nothing to the contrary.'

Despite this minor upset Adams was dutifully back at court the next day. His position was now positively humiliating, for the shogun was attending to no business more urgent than watching samurai at target practice. When a court official asked Adams why he was there and Adams replied that he came on behalf of the English captain — 'Why', said he, 'is he not gone'... and so went away laughing.'

A month after making their first application for an audience the English received a gift of twenty kimonos from the shogun, but no sign was given that the business of their embassy was to be considered. In disgust Cocks left Edo on 18 November, having accomplished nothing beyond a little sightseeing. Adams waited grimly on.

Hidetada's answer to the English complaint in fact came very shortly after Cocks's departure but gave no satisfaction. As the English ship had been taken outside Japanese waters, he declared the matter to be of no concern to him and therefore declined to take any measures against the Dutch.

Adams caught up with Cocks at Osaka and so shared with him the further humiliation heaped upon their party upon their return to Hirado — an ironic salute of welcome from the Dutch, fired off from the guns of their English prize.

22

'I William Adams mariner'

'I William Adams mariner that have been resident in Japan the space of some xviii or twenty years being sick in body but of a perfect rememberance laud and praise be unto Almighty God make and ordain this my present Testament...'
LAST WILL OF WILLIAM ADAMS, 16 MAY 1620

Despite the enmities and frustrations occasioned by the conflict between the English and the Dutch and the all but useless journey to Hidetada's court, Adams and Cocks continued to work closely together. One prize which had been won from the shogun was permission to make another trading voyage to Southeast Asia. It was decided on this occasion that the actual junk to be used would be a new one, belonging to a Japanese merchant, but that the Company would participate actively in the venture and that Adams would continue to serve as pilot.

Adams's last voyage began in mid-March 1619. The outward leg lasted a month, and the only incident worthy of note was the rescue of a fisherman. Adams's log book records that 'we saw a man upon a plank drowning... the which we made on board and saved by God's providence.' Arriving at Tonkin, the venturers landed their cargo, built some huts on shore and prudently surrounded them with a ditch and a palisade. Several days of wrangling followed, the merchants being reluctant to advance cash to the son of the local king before they had seen any of the silk they had come to buy. Eventually they agreed to do so, simply to avoid further delay. This soon proved to be an error of judgement, as compliance only brought further requests for cash in advance, 'but the merchants would deliver no more', and, after extensive and fruitless further negotiations through a eunuch intermediary, they went off to the capital to treat with the king's son in person.

The pilot meanwhile, set the crew to making ropes, cleaning and repairing the ship and redistributing its ballast. After several weeks of such time-filling activity Adams himself 'began to buy some merchandise'. When this led to 'some controversy' he and his companions retreated inside their compound and 'shut the gates... with out any further trouble'.

After this incident Adams kept the crew busy preparing the ship for the return voyage and, on his own initiative, sent its pinnace up river to the capital to fetch the king's son; but it returned the following day 'with a bad answer'. By now he was 'longing to hear from our merchants' and could have been little reassured by the arrival of 'one of the country people' who 'travelling in the night fell amongst thieves and was in divers parts wounded.' A week later came news that the merchants had been shipwrecked by a great storm. Two hours later they arrived safely with eight boats full of goods — but no silk. One final deputation went back to the capital to press the king's son to hand over the silk they had paid for. But they were to be disappointed — 'we had news we should have no silk of the king's son.' The return voyage began in mid-July. In the Straits of Hainan the ship struck a rock but was not badly damaged, 'thanks be to God for ever who preserved us miraculously'.

Adams arrived back at Hirado at the end of August. Shortly afterwards Cocks left to go to the court on business, but Adams did not follow him. Writing on 8 September, Eaton informed his senior colleague that he did not know 'when Capt. Addames will go up, in that he is sickly and minded to take physic'. Adams could not, however, have been seriously ill at that stage because just over a fortnight later Eaton wrote to tell Cocks that the pilot had helped two Englishmen, held captive aboard a Dutch man of war, to escape ashore and find refuge in the English house. Cocks's correspondence also shows that Adams was actively involved in commercial dealings as late as February 1620; and that his services were still valued may be seen from the satisfaction with which Cocks recorded the failure of a local Japanese official, 'a large mouthed man' who 'would if he could, set debate betwixt Capt. Adames and us, but it is not in his power to do it'. That Adams had lost none of his sea-faring skill is also testified by Cocks's report that when he and Adams had been journeying along the coast in a couple of open boats 'we had sixteen oars to row but... Capt. Adams with half the number out-rowed us at his pleasure.'

Adams's death, therefore, seems to have come suddenly upon him, for Cocks later gives the date of his demise as the date upon which his last will was made — 16 May 1620. There were six English witnesses to the document and this fact, together with Adams's rescue of the two Englishmen from the Dutch ship and the fact that the benefactions in his will were all made to Englishmen and Japanese show that, although he may have become a 'naturalized Japanner', he was far from having been 'Hollandized'.

Adams divided the main part of his estate into two equal parts, half going to his family in England and half to his family in Japan. Cocks, as one of the two executors, later made it clear to the relevant authorities in England that Mrs. Adams was to have only half of what Adams had bequeathed, the other half being paid direct to her offspring 'for it was not his mind his wife should have all, in regard she might marry an other husband and carry all'. Mrs. Adams also secured, in October 1621, the pilot's English property, valued at £165. And it is likely that she did marry again, for the parish register of St. Dunstan's Stepney, contains entries for the remarriage of two widows called Mary Adams, one in 1627 and another in 1629. Of Adams's daughter, Deliverance, there is only a bare mention in the East India Company records that in 1624 she lodged a petition in respect of her father's estate. Coupled with the fact of the probable remarriage of Mrs. Adams this suggests that the pilot's twenty-year separation from his first wife had done little to change his assessment of her character and therefore clearly explains the precautions he took with regard to the distribution of that part of his legacy.

Little is known of the subsequent history of Adams's Japanese family. Hidetada confirmed the son, Joseph, in the inheritance of his estate within the year and Cocks handed over to him, according to Adams's direction, the pilot's swords — 'where were tears shed at delivery'. The acquisition of an estate and the assumption of samurai rank did not, however, turn Joseph into a landed gentleman. Instead he chose to follow his father's calling as a pilot and in that capacity made at least five voyages to Southeast Asia between 1624 and 1635. Like a dutiful son, he built a shrine at Hemimura to the memory of his parents, Magome having died there in 1634. Of daughter Susanna's later life nothing is known beyond the fact that in 1622 Cocks, who was very fond of her, sent her a gift of fancy cloth. Equally obscure is the fate of Adams's third, illegitimate child, who was born at Hirado and passes unmentioned in his will. In February 1621 Cocks recorded in his diary that 'Capt. Adames child in Firando was brought to me per the mother, unto whom I gave two tais in small plate [i.e. about ten shillings] and offered her to pay for the bringing of it up to school, if she would deliver it to the English nation's protection.'

Presumably she did not, because the only other entry referring to the child, in April of the same year, simply records payment for a piece of 'Japon taffety' to line its coat.

To Cocks himself Adams left his celestial globe, his sea-charts and his best sword — in other words his most prized personal possessions. To Eaton he gave his books and navigational instruments, and to each of four other Englishmen he bequeathed 'one Kerrymon [i.e. kimono] of the best I have'. His Japanese servants received various sums of money, as did his long-time landlord at Hirado, Yasemon Dono.

Cock's genuine affection for Adams, despite their differences, cannot be doubted. He had long maintained an independent correspondence with Adams's family and continued to interest himself in their welfare after the pilot's death. Nor was he in any doubt regarding Adams's standing in his adopted country, and the opinion he expressed on that subject in a letter to the directors of the East India Company might well stand as the fitting epitaph to the pilot's unique career:

'I cannot but be sorrowful for the loss of such a man as Capt. Wm. Adames was, he having been in such favour with two emperors of Japan as never was any Christian in these parts of the world, and might freely have entered and had speech with the emperors, when many Japon kings stood without and could not be permitted.'

Adams's merit was likewise acknowledged by his faraway countrymen, and he was, a generation after his death, famous enough to be celebrated in Thomas Fuller's *Worthies of England:*

'In order to the settlement of trade [Adams] endured many miseries. He who reads them will concur with Cato and repent that he ever went there by sea, whither one might go by land. But Japan being an island, and inaccessible save by sea, our Adams his discretion [i.e. decision] was not to be blamed but industry to be commended in his adventures.'

23

'out of hope'

'And truly to my heart's grief I am every day more than other out of hope of any good to be done in Japoñ.'
LETTER OF RICHARD COCKS TO THE EAST INDIA COMPANY, 10 MARCH 1620

The closing months of Adams's life were clouded by the outbreak of open violence between the Dutch and the English at Hirado. The Dutch came to seize by force the men that Adams had helped to escape from their custody, along with four others who had also managed to break free. Cocks later described the incident in a letter to the directors of the East India Company:

'they came on shore by multitudes, thinking by force to have entered in our house and cut all our throats, giving three assaults in one day. Yet the Japons took our parts, that they could do us no harm, although there were five or six hundred of them, against five or six persons of us. And the next day morning after... a company of them entered our house... where they wounded John Coaker and an other, thinking they had killed one of them at least, as they made their brags after. So that we were constrained to keep in our house a guard of Japons, night and day.'

In the same letter Cocks also mentioned the kidnap of one of his men and unprovoked firing on an English junk by Dutch shore battery. But the main burden of his tale was a lengthy explanation of the unprofitability of the English factory. He laid the blame on many factors — the expensive and unlucky voyages to Southeast Asia, the low state of the Japanese market, the rapacious efforts of Japanese merchants to squeeze out foreigners, the indifference of the local people to English broadcloth, the poor health of his colleagues, the unsuitability of the harbour at Hirado compared with Nagasaki and, not least, the greediness of the local daimyo and his officials. The relative success of the Dutch, who faced many of the same difficulties, was explained away by the privileged position they were able to buy for themselves through lavish bribery financed by the spoils of their privateering. Cocks's formidable catalogue of excuses also included, significantly, a rebuttal of rumours that he had been keeping false accounts and living as a 'gamester or riotous person' and ended with an all but open appeal for sympathy that he should 'lie in a place of much loss and expense to your worships and no benefit to myself, but loss of time in my old age.'

Long before he received a reply to his letter Cocks's topsy-turvy world took a new tilt in a quite unexpected direction. In August 1620 there arrived at Hirado a joint Anglo-Dutch expeditionary force, euphemistically called the 'Fleet of Defence', but explicitly intended, as a result of an alliance sealed in London in June of the previous year, to prey upon Spanish and Portuguese shipping in Far Eastern waters. Henceforth the English and the Dutch in Japan were to be the best of friends — by order. And so they became, to all outward intents and purposes, explaining their sudden reconciliation to Hidetada in the most high-minded and patriotic — but scarcely plausible — terms, as the outcome of an inspired and unselfish desire to smite down the overweening power of the King of Spain.

The alliance prospered to the extent that the Spanish and Portuguese were harried unmercifully and the English factory waxed at least a little fat on its share of the prizes. But the division of the spoils led to many quarrels, often bloody ones; and the drunken brawls and thefts of the sea-rovers when in port provoked much wrath from the local forces of law and order. After two years the alliance ended. The news of its termination brought no relief to Cocks but rather the reverse, for it was accompanied by a starkly worded order to close down the Hirado factory and report to English headquarters at Batavia in Indonesia to answer charges of incompetence and loose living. Cocks demurred on the grounds — all too true — that he still needed time in Japan to wind up the Company's affairs. In May 1623, however a special emissary arrived to implement the closure order and bring back Cocks and his companions, by force if necessary.

The more or less sudden departure of the English allowed large numbers of Japanese noblemen to renege on their debts to the Company, thereby plunging Cocks even deeper into disgrace. At Batavia he was roundly condemned for 'insufferable neglects and abuses' — his failure to prevent his colleagues from engaging in private trading on their own account, his over-generous expenditures on food and drink for the English household and its guests and employees, his persisting vulnerability to the wiles of the

Chinese merchants, who took his gifts but never actually helped him get into the China trade, and lastly his inability to keep any sort of organized and systematic accounts. Cocks left Batavia bound for London and a full enquiry at the hands of the court of directors. But he died long before reaching his destination, and, having been buried at sea, was spared the humiliation which his easy-going nature had brought upon him.

If he had had the spirit to argue his case Cocks might well have pointed out that his Dutch rivals had regularly received both moral and material support, both from home and from other parts of their maritime trading empire, whereas he had been obliged to soldier on for up to three years at a time without sight of an English ship, and he might also have pointed out how the Company had doomed itself to a decade of failure at the very outset, when Saris ignored Adams's advice and chose to site its main base of operations not at Uraga, in the shadow of the shogun's court, but far away in Hirado, under the very noses of the Dutch.

And so the English departed. A year after they went the Spanish were ordered out. In 1639 the Portuguese were expelled. Only the Dutch remained, confined to a tiny artificial island in the harbour of Nagasaki — without freedom, without honour, but not without profit.

24

Epilogue

Exactly fifty years after the closure of the English factory at Hirado an East India Company ship with, in the circumstances, the entirely appropriate name of *Return,* came to Nagasaki with a message from Charles II calling for the restoration of the trade link which had been established sixty years earlier in the reign of his grandfather, James I. But the request was rejected, possibly because the Japanese learned that Charles was married to Catherine of Braganza, a Portuguese Catholic princess.

In 1808 the frigate *Phaeton* entered Nagasaki harbour under a Dutch flag to ask for supplies. The local governor, mortified at this violation of the official policy of seclusion, committed suicide.

Trading links between Britain and Japan were finally restored half a century after this untoward incident, Commodore Matthew Perry and the US Navy having blazed the way — or threatened to.

Within a little more than a decade the Japanese authorities had determined upon a policy of rapid 'modernization'. To create western-style institutions, based on the latest technology, it proved necessary to import some hundreds of 'honourable foreign experts', more derogatorily referred to in the vernacular as *yatoi* — 'live machines'. More than half of them were British and, as such, they followed in the footsteps of that first and most versatile of British *yatoi*: William Adams, shipwright, map-maker, gunner, interpreter, diplomat, business man, teacher of mathematics — and pilot.

British involvement in Japan not unnaturally led to a revival of interest in the personality and career of the once celebrated, but by Victorian times scarcely remembered, pilot. The tombs on a hill in Hemimura which are reputed to be those of Adams and his wife (Adams may actually be buried at Hirado) were rediscovered in 1872 by an English merchant and in 1905, in the presence of Prince Arthur of Connaught, became designated as an official memorial. Anjin-cho, a street in Tokyo's Nihonbashi district where Adams once owned a house, also preserved his memory in this period. In 1918 he was further memorialized by a commemorative stone pillar, bearing a lengthy account of his career, which was erected in a park at Hemi.

Proposals by the Japan Society around the beginning of the present century to erect a similar monument at Adams's birthplace, Gillingham, Kent, evoked 'but a luke-warm interest' and it was not until 1934 that a clock-tower was erected by public subscription to that end and inaugurated in the presence of the then Japanese ambassador and other dignitaries.

In 1947, in the presence of the Commander-in-chief of the British Commonwealth Forces of Occupation in Japan, another memorial to William Adams was unveiled at Ito, a town on the seacoast south of Tokyo. A poem in his honour, by Edmund Blunden, was later inscribed on a stone tablet and placed beside it. Each year since then a memorial ceremony has been held at Ito in honour of the pilot, usually in the presence of diplomatic and naval personnel from Britain, the Netherlands and the United States. It is believed that Adams did his ship-building for the shogun in this vicinity.

Gillingham and Yokosuka, the administrative area which embraces Hemi and Ito, also maintain a 'twinning' relationship and the schools of the two communities exchange examples of their pupils' work from time to time.

A Note on Sources and Further Reading

William Adams's letters are reproduced in *Memorials of the Empire of Japon*, edited by Thomas Rundall and published by the Hakluyt Society in 1850. This volume also contains the first description of Japan ever published in English. *The Voyage of Captain John Saris to Japan 1613*, edited by Sir Ernest Satow, was published by the Hakluyt Society in 1900; this volume also contains an account of the early development of English commerce in the Far East as well as much biographical information about Saris himself. Richard Cocks's *Diary* was also published by the Hakluyt Society in two volumes in 1883. A three-volume edition was published by the Historiographical Institute of the University of Tokyo in 1979–80; this also contains the letters Cocks sent during the period from February 1619 to December 1620 when the diary is blank. An extensive collection of relevant materials was compiled as a *History of Japan* by an East India Company employee, Peter Pratt, in 1822; it was subsequently edited by M. Paske-Smith, published at Kobe in 1931 and republished in London by the Curzon Press in 1972. Adams's log-books for the voyages he made between 1614 and 1619 are preserved in the Bodleian Library; a transcript, edited by C. J. Purnell, was published in Vol. XIII of the *Transactions and Proceedings of the Japan Society of London*. A rather general sketch, 'In Memory of Will Adams, the First Englishman in Japan', by A. Diosy, with some useful bibliographic references, can be found in Vol. VI of the same publication. In Vol. XXVI of the *Transactions of the Asiatic Society of Japan* can be found L. Riess's 'History of the English Factory at Hirado'.

An extensive narrative of events, with lengthy quotations from original sources, can be found in Murdoch and Yamagata's *A History of Japan During the Century of Early Foreign Intercourse* published in 1925 (see especially Vol. II). The standard account remains Sir George Sansom's classic three-volume *A History of Japan* published by the Cresset Press in 1961. A thematic selection of documentary materials can be found in Michael Cooper's entertaining *They Came to Japan: An Anthology of European Reports on Japan 1543–1640,* published by Thames and Hudson in 1965; see also the same author's lavishly illustrated *'The Southern Barbarians: The First Europeans in Japan,* published by Kodansha International in 1971. The standard biography of Ieyasu is still A. L. Sadler's *The Maker of Modern Japan,* published by Allen and Unwin in 1937. Other relevant works include C. R. Boxer's *The Christian Century in Japan 1549–1650* (1951), Sir George Sansom's *The Western World and Japan* (1950), P. G. Rogers *The First Englishman in Japan* (1956) and Peter Duus's *Feudalism in Japan* (1969).

Adams's story has long attracted the interest of writers of historical fiction. As far back as 1861 William Dalton wrote *Will Adams: The First Englishman in Japan: A Romantic Biography.* In the 1930s there appeared J. A. B. Scherer's *Pilot and Shogun: A Story of Old Japan* and Richard Blaker's *The Needle-Watcher,* the latter being reprinted in 1973 for a new generation of readers. In that same year there appeared Christopher Nicole's *Lord of the Golden Fan.* The latest phase in the cycle is represented by James Clavell's massive *Shōgun,* whose hero, John Blackthorne, is but a thinly disguised figuration of the original William Adams, though his career is somewhat more fantastic — if that were possible.

For a critical review of the various William Adams novels, of Shogun and the film and TV series based on it, see Henry B. Smith (ed), *Learning from Shōgun: Japanese History & Western Fantasy* Paul Norbury Publications 1982.

Tea bowl of the mid seventeenth century.

William Adams and His World: A Comparative Chronology

		England & Europe	Japan
1564	Birth of William Adams	Birth of Shakespeare	Spanish occupy the Philippines
1565			
1566			
1567			
1568			Nobunaga becomes supreme in Japan
1569		Mercator publishes map of the world	
1570			Nagasaki opened to foreign trade
1571		Battle of Lepanto breaks Turkish sea-power in the Mediterranean. Dutch War of liberation against Spanish rule begins	
1573			End of Ashikaga shogunate
1574			
1575		Sir Humphrey Gilbert advocates English colonization	Battle of Nagashino, massive use of firearms
1576	Adams apprenticed		Azuchi Castle begun

1577	First account of Japan in English	Alliance of England and Netherlands	
1578			
1579			
1580		Drake completes voyage around the world	
		Spain annexes Portugal	
1581			
1582		Gregorian calendar introduced	Death of Nobunaga
1583		Newfoundland becomes England's first colony	Osaka Castle begun
1584		Raleigh claims Virginia for England	Hideyoshi supreme in Japan
1585			
1586			
1587		Drake attacks Cadiz	Sword hunt disarms peasantry
			First persecution of Christians
1588	Adams commands *Richard Duffield*	Defeat of Spanish Armada	
1589	Adams marries Mary Hyn		
1590			Unification of Japan completed
1591	First English voyage to the East Indies		
1592			Japanese invasion of Korea
1593	Adams sails to discover N.E. passage		Japanese retreat in Korea

1594		Dutch send ships direct to Asia	
1595			
1596		Galileo invents thermometer	
1597			Execution of 26 Christians
1598	Adams leaves England		Death of Hideyoshi
1599	Adams passes Straits of Magellan		
1600	Adams arrives in Japan	Founding of East India Company	
1601		Van Noort completes the 4th voyage round the world	
1602	Crew of the *Liefde* disperse		
1603		James I succeeds Elizabeth I	Ieyasu becomes shogun
1604		Peace between England & Spain Jesuits banished from England	
1605		Gunpowder plot	Hidetada becomes shogun
1606		Anti-Catholic laws in England	Anti-Christian decrees proclaimed
1607		First permanent English settlement in Virginia	
1608	Adams's mission to the Philippines	Invention of the telescope	
1609	Shipwreck of Don Rodrigo		Dutch arrive in Nagasaki and set up factory at Hirado
1610			

1611	Adams negotiates on behalf of the Dutch	Colonization of Ulster	
1612			Persecution of Christian missionaries
1613	Adams is employed by the East India Company		First English ship arrives in Japan
1614	Adams's first voyage in the *Sea Adventure*		Siege of Osaka Castle
1615	Adams's second voyage in the *Sea Adventure*		Fall of Osaka Castle
			'Laws of the Military Houses issued'
1616		Death of Shakespeare	Death of Ieyasu
1617	Adams's voyage in the *Gift of God*	Raleigh's last voyage	
1618		Raleigh executed Thirty Years War begins	
1619	Adam's last voyage		
1620	Death of William Adams	Pilgrim Fathers sail to America	Anglo-Dutch alliance